本书获"东华大学研究生课程(教材)建设项目经费"资助

英汉汉英散文翻译与评析
Translation and Comments of English and Chinese Essays

唐　毅　顾韶阳　**译著**

东南大学出版社
SOUTHEAST UNIVERSITY PRESS
·南京·

图书在版编目(CIP)数据

英汉汉英散文翻译与评析／唐毅,顾韶阳译著．
南京：东南大学出版社,2020.6(2024.2 重印)
 ISBN 978-7-5641-8820-7

Ⅰ.①英⋯ Ⅱ.①唐⋯ ②顾⋯ Ⅲ.①散文-英语-文学翻译-研究 Ⅳ.①H315.9

中国版本图书馆 CIP 数据核字(2020)第 013473 号

本书部分文字作品稿酬已委托中国文字著作权协会转付,敬请相关著作权人联系：
电话:010-65978917,传真:010-65978926,E-mail：Wenzhuxie@126.com

英汉汉英散文翻译与评析 Yinghan Hanying Sanwen Fanyi Yu Pingxi

译　著　唐毅　顾韶阳	责任编辑　刘　坚
电　话　(025)83793329　QQ:635353748	电子邮件　liu-jian@ seu.edu.cn
出版发行　东南大学出版社	出 版 人　江建中
地　址　南京市四牌楼 2 号(210096)	邮　编　210096
销售电话　(025)83794561/83794174/83794121/83795801/83792174/83795802/57711295(传真)	
网　址　http://www.seupress.com	电子邮件　press@ seupress.com
经　销　全国各地新华书店	印　刷　广东虎彩云印刷有限公司
开　本　787mm×1092mm　1/16	印　张　10.25　字　数　245 千字
版　次　2020 年 6 月第 1 版	印　次　2024 年 2 月第 2 次印刷
书　号　ISBN 978-7-5641-8820-7	
定　价　45.00 元	

＊未经许可,本书内文字不得以任何方式转载、演绎,违者必究。
＊本社图书若有印装质量问题,请直接与营销部联系。电话:025-83791830。

序

  韶阳邀我为这本《英汉汉英散文翻译与评析》写个序,我很乐意,甚至心里还有点儿喜滋滋的,因为英语文学和文字,以及两种文字转换的翻译,既是我的专业,又是我的喜好。我要写序,就必须从终日穷忙的匆忙中挤出一大块时间,静下心来,认真研读精选的散文,那是一些随处可见修辞、气韵、性情、言志、明道的散文,一些描写入微、回味无穷的散文,它们可以给我的精神添一份食粮,给我增加一份对人生的洞察力,给我时不时冒出来的怪念头增加一份理解力。同时,我还可以学习一下同行的文学鉴赏力以及转换文字技艺,先于他人享受一下译者禀赋、才能和素养所带给读者的快乐。

  这本集子分两大部分,第一部分是英译汉,这部分的翻译和评说主要由唐毅承担,第二部分是汉译英,这部分的翻译和评说主要由顾韶阳承担。根据我自己有限的经验,英译汉的译文若要够味,尽如人意,译者必须有极高的中文造诣。对照英语原文,我觉得,唐毅老师在理解英语原文的表面意义及深层意义基础上,将自己的译文处理得看上去似乎亦步亦趋,但却非常流畅,没有丝毫的"硬邦邦"的翻译腔,读起来似乎是原作一般,行云流水,一气呵成。据此,我觉得她是一个中文很有修养的学者。下面我随意摘取两段文字,供大家欣赏:(1)"它在薄雾朦胧的清晨无声无息地潜入,又在阳光和煦的午后悄然消失了踪影。它踮起脚尖,轻手轻脚地掠过树顶,顺手抹红了几片叶子,又踏着一丛蓟花冠毛,越过峡谷后飘然而去。它时而坐在山巅,咕咕声犹如十月黄昏中鸣叫的猫头鹰,时而又和风儿追逐玩耍。九月又是变化无常的。它一会儿繁忙得如同山核桃树上的小松鼠,一会儿又慵懒得有如缓缓流淌的小溪。夏季的成熟与丰饶成就了甜美的九月。"(摘自《甜美的九月》)(2)"真正的友谊是慢慢生长起来的,只有彼此了解、互有美德,友谊之树才会枝繁叶茂。年轻人之间还有一种名不符实的友谊,热络一时,但幸好并不长久。他们偶然相逢,因聚众闹事、寻欢作乐而匆匆结缘成为朋友。这种因酒色而更加牢固的'美好'友谊,其实就是沆瀣一气。"(摘自《切斯费尔德勋爵的〈致子书〉》)

  若是汉译英,理解一般不是大问题,英语表达却可能纷然杂陈,优等与劣等的译文可以相差十万八千里。韶阳的英语译文不仅规范,而且有不少可点可圈的出彩地方,这里仅举三个例子:(1) 朱光潜写的散文《无所为而为》,其题目是从老子的思想中得来的启示,有点儿抽象,文字读起来虽然似乎上口,却又给人一种异常的感觉。译者不甘心单单将内在意思在译文中表现出来,一定要在"形神"方面给一个与原文匹配的译文:Being Purposive without

Purpose。这里，虽然 purposive 比较生僻，却与后面的 purpose 压了头韵，对应了原文的"为……为"的结构，且意思非常接近原文。我觉得这是一个很好的尝试，尽管可能有人会提出质疑。(2) 就在这篇散文中有这么一句话："人要有出世的精神才可以做入世的事业"，翻译处理是："Only with an outlook of other-worldliness can one achieve this-worldly success."译者将"出世"用复合词"other-worldliness"来表达，而"入世的"则用复合词"this-worldly"来表达，既有"创作性"，又合乎英语习惯，因为 other-worldly 常常表示"非世俗的"的意思，比如：西方人对《庄子》中的"抱柱之信"的评论是"the other-worldly nature of the woman's love"。(3) 下面的例子取自钱锺书的"《人兽鬼》序"的最后一句话："我不敢梦想我的艺术会那么成功，惟有事先否认，并且敬谢他抬举我的好意。"英语译文是："I dare not dream of such artistic attainments, so I have to decline politely in advance this undeserved flattery."这里，我评说两点，第一，"艺术成功"翻译处理为"artistic attainments"，符合英语搭配的习惯。若这一点是基本要求，不值得大赞，那么第二点却值得激赏了，即将"敬谢他抬举我的好意"翻译成"decline politely this underserved flattery"，其中，短语 this undeserved flattery 曲尽其妙，将作者表面上谦卑、实际上讽刺的含义淋漓尽致地表达了出来。

  韶阳是我的学生，喜好英语文字，见到我就想聊英语，聊到兴奋时常常到了忘我的境界。今天，他那些硬底子的英语想必是长期付出辛劳、奋勉努力的结果。英语学习没有止境，希望韶阳百丈竿头，更进一步，取得新成绩。

史志康
上海外国语大学教授、博导
2020 年 5 月

第一部分　英译汉

Sweet September
　/甜美的九月 ··· 1

Singing, Each to Each
　/你吟我唱 ·· 7

First Snow
　/初　雪 ··· 11

Appetite
　/欲　望 ··· 15

Lord Chesterfield's Letter to His Son
　/切斯费尔德勋爵的《致子书》 ·· 20

On Doors
　/门之思 ··· 26

Domestick Greatness Unattainable
　/近观无伟人 ··· 31

Kunqu Opera, *The Peony Pavilion*
　/昆曲《牡丹亭》 ··· 37

The Rose
　/那株蔷薇 ··· 44

How We Kept Mother's Day
　/我们怎样庆祝母亲节 ·· 50

On Poverty
　/论贫穷 ··· 58

On Man's Extravagance
/论男人的奢侈 65

The Wife
/妻 子 72

The Drawing-Room
/客 厅 79

Is Love an Art?
/爱是一门艺术吗? 84

第二部分 汉译英

无所为而为
/Being Purposive without Purpose 92

往 事
/Memories 95

寂 寞
/Loneliness 98

伤 逝
/Remembering the Departed Friends 103

钱锺书序两则
/Two Prefaces by Qian Zhongshu 109

窗 帘
/Window Curtains 113

爱
/Love 117

成 功
/Success 120

朋友四型
/Four Categories of Friends 125

留住文字的绿意
/ Retaining the Green through Words ·· 130

在敦煌时是与历史最亲近的时刻
/ When in Dunhuang He Was Closest to History ································ 135

那一刻，我看到了人性的光辉
/ That moment, I glimpsed the glow of humanity ································ 139

细　艺
/ Minor Hobbies ·· 143

知　止
/ Knowing When to Stop ·· 147

雪与炉火
/ Snow and Stove Fire ·· 151

Sweet September
甜 美 的 九 月

By *Hal Borland*
文/哈尔·白兰德　译/唐毅

译者按：哈尔·白兰德（1900—1978），美国作家、记者、自然主义者。在《甜美的九月》一文中，作者用非常优美的语言，展示了一幅秋景图：林木葱茏、秋叶斑斓、鲜花绽放、动物嬉戏、农人忙碌。作者的观察细致入微，从花草、林木到空气、气味，作者全方位展示了秋天的美丽景象。就翻译而言，译者需要把握好直译和意译的关系，把握词义的虚实转换，将文中一些较为抽象、语义较为模糊的词语具体、准确地翻译出来。此外，译者也应充分利用汉语意合的特点，使译文灵动飘逸，更好地呈现如诗如画的秋景。

September is more than a month, really; it is a season, an achievement in itself. It begins with August's leftovers[1] and it ends with October's preparations[2], but along the way it achieves special satisfactions. After summer's heat and haste, the year consolidates itself. Deliberate September—in its own time and tempo—begins to sum up another summer.

With September comes a sense of autumn. It creeps in on a misty dawn and vanishes in the

九月绝不仅仅是一个月份，她是一个季节，一个收获的季节。九月初始于八月的余音，终结于十月的繁忙。一路走来，她怡然自得，收获满满。经过了夏季的炎热和躁动，一年开始沉静下来，为来年的繁荣做准备。九月，踏着自己的节拍，从容地宣告又一个夏季的结束。

九月给我们带来了丝丝的秋意。它在薄雾朦胧的清晨无声无息地潜入，又在

hot afternoon. It tiptoes through the treetops, rouging a few leaves, then rides a tuft of thistle down across the valley and away³. It sits on a hilltop and hoots like an October owl in the dusk. It plays tag with the wind. September is a changeling⁴ busy as a squirrel in a hickory tree, idle as a languid brook. It is summer's ripeness and richness fulfilled.

Some of the rarest days of the year come in the September season—days when it is comfortably cold but pulsing with life, when the sky is clear and clean, the air crisp, the wind free of dust. Meadows still smell of hay and the sweetness of cut grass. September flowers are less varied than those of May but so abundant that they make September another flowery month. Goldenrod comes by mid-August, but rises to a peak of golden abundance in early September. Late thistles make spectacular purple accents. And asters blossom everywhere, along the roadsides, in meadows, on the hilltops, even in city lots, ranging in color from pure white through all degrees of lavender to the royal New England purple⁵.

We think of spring as the miracle time, when opening bud and new leaf proclaim the persistence of life. But September is when the abiding wonder makes itself known in a subtler way⁶. Now growth comes to annual fruition, and preparations are completed for another

阳光和煦的午后悄然消失了踪影。它踮起脚尖，轻手轻脚地掠过树顶，顺手抹红了几片叶子，又踏着一丛蓟花冠毛，越过峡谷后飘然而去。它时而坐在山巅，咕咕声犹如十月黄昏中鸣叫的猫头鹰，时而又和风儿追逐玩耍。九月又是变化无常的。它一会儿繁忙得如同山核桃树上的小松鼠，一会儿又慵懒得有如缓缓流淌的小溪。夏季的成熟与丰饶成就了甜美的九月。

一年中难得的几天好时光就在九月到来。九月天气凉爽宜人，万物生机勃勃。天空清澈明澄，空气清冽，纤尘不染。草地上飘散着干草味和新割下的草的甜甜的气息。九月的花儿虽不如五月的花儿那样百花争艳，但各色花儿将九月装扮成又一个花季。金菊八月中旬含苞，九月初即绽放。晚蓟花开，紫色一片，蔚为壮观。紫菀怒放，道路边，草地上，山顶上，甚或是都市的空地上，处处可见芳踪。千姿百态、素白、淡紫、深紫，色彩丰富，有的平易如薰衣草，有的高贵如皇室紫，斑斓绚丽。

春季蓓蕾绽放，新叶吐绿，生机盎然。春天是一个昭示生命奇迹的季节，而秋天则以其婉约之姿展示这个奇迹。九月，生长，成熟，不仅一年的硕果尽在于此，它又为来年、新生的生命做好准备。橡果熟了，胡桃老了。植物将未来托付给种子和

year, another generation. The acorn ripens and the hickory nut matures. The plant commits its future to the seed and the root. The insect stows tomorrow in the egg and the pupa. The surge is almost over and life begins to relax.

  The green prime is passing. The trees begin to proclaim the change. Soon the leaves will be discarded, the grass will sere[7]. But the miracle of life persists, the mysterious germ of growth and renewal that is the seed itself.

  This is the season of the harvest moon. With reasonably clear skies it will be a moonlit week, for the harvest moon is not hasty; it comes early and stays late. There was a time when the busy farmer could return to the fields after supper and continue his harvest by moonlight. There's still harvesting to be done, but much of it now centers on the kitchen rather than the barns. The last bountiful yield comes from the garden, the late sweet corn, the tomatoes, the root vegetables. The canning, the preserving, the freezing, the kitchen harvest in all its variety, reaches its peak.

  First frost comes in the night, a clear, scant-starred night when the moon is near its fullness. It comes without a whisper, quiet as thistledown, brushing the corner of a hillside garden. Dawn comes and you see its path—the glistening leaf, the gleaming stem, the limp, blackening garden vine.

  Another night or two the frost walks the

根茎，昆虫将明天托付给卵蛹。勃发的生命脉动接近尾声，开始歇息。

  绿色葱茏即将逝去，叶落，草枯。季节的更替在树木的身上一览无余。可是，生命的奇迹生生不息，成长与重生就孕育在神秘的粒粒种籽中。

  九月是收获的季节。天空明净，持续数日。夜晚月光皎洁，月儿早早升上天空，迟迟离去，淡定从容。忙碌的农夫吃完晚饭，又回到田间地头，顶着月光收割。农夫还有好多事要做，活儿只不过从谷场移到了厨房。菜园里晚熟的玉米、西红柿、根茎类蔬菜，是丰收的最后一批果实。在厨房里，该罐装的罐装，该腌制的腌制，该冷冻的冷冻，好一派热闹忙碌的景象。

  月儿快要满盈的时候，月明星稀，初霜降临。它掠过山边的菜园，静如蓟花般悄然而至。晨曦初露，树叶上、树干上、藤蔓上，点点霜花，晶莹闪烁。

  再过一两天，霜花借着月色，来到

valleys in the moonlight. Then it goes back beyond the northern hills to wait a little longer, and the golden mildness of early autumn comforts the land. A faint anise smell is on the air, goldenrod scent. The mist swirls and September sun shines through the deep-blue sky of September[8].

To warm-blooded creatures, the crisp, cool nights of September are invigorating. But cold-blooded insects are at the mercy of the sun and now their clocks run down. The cicada is stilled. The chorus of the cricket and katydid diminishes. When they rasp at all it is with the deliberate tempo of a fiddler drawing a worn bow across fraying strings.

Now come the hoarding days. Mice have been harvesting and stowing seeds for weeks[9]. The chipmunk lines his winter bedroom, and squirrels hid the nut trees' bounty. The woodchucks, gorging on grass and clover and fruit, lay up their harvest in body fat under their own skins.

The flickers begin to gather for migration. All summer these big wood-peckers were resolutely individual, busy with family life and wanting no company. Now they are gregarious, with time for tribal gossip and community play. The warblers and swallows have already formed inpremigration flocks; soon the robins will be gathering too. Nesting is completed, fledglings are on their own, and there is food in plenty.

山谷,然后越过北坡回来小憩。初秋金色的太阳暖暖地照耀着大地,空气中飘散着淡淡的茴香和金菊的香气。薄雾漫舞,天空湛蓝,九月暖阳,万千闪耀。

对于温血动物来讲,清冷的九月夜晚依然生机勃勃,而冷血动物失去了太阳的庇护,生命的时钟开始了倒计时。蝉儿静了,蟋蟀和蚱蜢的合唱息了。虽然它们还会吟唱,可这吟唱宛如一个小提琴手小心翼翼地用破旧的琴弓在松弛的琴弦上发出的喑哑琴声。

储藏的季节到了。田鼠采集果实,储存种子,忙活了数周。金花鼠将种子堆满了过冬的洞穴,松鼠将胡桃树的果实收藏了起来。土拨鼠拼命吃下青草、三叶草和果实,将吃下的东西储存在皮下厚厚的脂肪中。

候鸟开始集结迁徙。整整一个夏季,这些大大的啄木鸟忙着各自享受家庭生活,并不想彼此结伴。现在,它们聚在一起,彼此闲聊,集体玩耍。鸣鸟和燕子已经排好了迁徙飞行的队列,很快知更鸟也将加入其中。窝筑好了,幼鸟自己觅食,食物充足。九月就是鸟儿的假期。谁知道它们是不是在讨论即将开始的旅行呢?

Sweet September

September is vacation time for birds. Who knows but that they are discussing the trip ahead?

By September's end the treasure chest of autumn begins to "spill over" with wealth. You see it glowing in the quiet afternoon, aflame in the sunset.

Woodland, roadside and dooryard will soon be jeweled beyond a rajah's richest dreams.

The year's season in the sun has run its course. Nature begins to prepare for winter. After the color in the woodlands, the leaves will blanket the soil. The litter of autumn will become mulch, then humus for root and tender seed. The urgency of growth is ended for another year, but life itself is hoarded in root and bulb and seed and egg.

秋天收获的宝藏太多,在九月末开始满溢。这些宝藏在寂静的午后,在日落的余晖中,熠熠发光。

林地、路边、门前小院,很快将被秋色点缀得一片珠光宝气,即使古印度王侯最美的梦也梦不到这番景象。

秋季在阳光下走完了它的行程。大自然开始为越冬做准备。林地里斑斓的叶片将为大地铺上一层厚毯。掉落的秋叶将化为护根,继而化为腐殖质,为根茎和柔嫩的种子提供来年的养分。生长停歇,静待来年,而生命就藏在根与球茎中,藏在卵与种子中。

注释:

1. leftovers 可指"残羹剩饭",也可以是"剩余物"之意。从语境来看,取"剩余物"之意比较恰当。此词在这里的意思是指自然万物经历了火热八月(夏季),旺盛的生命力在秋季开始衰减,故而译为"余音"这样语意美好的词义。

2. 此词看似简单,其实不然。如果直接译为"准备",会造成译而不达的后果。其实通过上下文,我们可以看出,这里的"preparation"意指十月是收获的季节,大自然经过春季播种、夏季生长、秋季成熟、冬季凋零的历程。因此,这里的"preparation"就是为秋天收获而做的准备,收获时节也是十分忙碌的季节,因此译为"繁忙"。

3. 作者在此运用了拟人的手法,把金秋当作一个顽皮的孩童来描写,译者需要充分表现出这一写作手法。为此,此段落中的一些关键字词,如"tiptoes"(踮起脚尖)、"rouging"(顺手抹红)、"rides"(踏着)这些动词,译者都将动作具体地译出。一些介词,如"through" "across""away",译者也采用词性转换的手法,译为动词,以符合顽皮孩童嬉戏的形象。通过描绘动作,一是忠实地呈现了原作中的修辞手法,二是十分生动地描绘出了初秋刚至的景象。

4. 查阅字典可知"changeling"一词意为"矮小丑陋的小孩,低能儿"。照此意思翻译,自然难以理解。通过上下文可知,九月是多变的季节,时而慵懒,时而繁忙。所以可以确定,changeling 在此应是"changeable"的意思。这也与此词的古用法"善变的人"一致。

5. 此句原文比较简洁,译者通过增词的手法,将层次丰富的紫色表现出来。原文"ranging"一词表明这里的紫色的色彩层次分明,浅淡深浓都有,因此译文就将原文中没有具体描绘的不同层次的色彩呈现出来:"素白、淡紫、深紫"。另外,在西方人们通常认为紫色是高贵的色彩,通常王室或教会上层都会运用紫色以示显贵,与中国皇帝使用黄色以表尊贵是一个道理。所以译者根据语境,加上"平易"和"高贵"一对反义词,来突出紫色的丰富多变。

6. 按照英文写作的习惯,可以是先概括,再具体说明。此段写春、秋两季的景致就是如此。译者在此为了突出春秋不同的景致,对语篇做了调整,将具体说明春景的"春季蓓蕾绽放,新叶吐绿,生机盎然"单独译出,放在段首,然后将原文首句的主句分拆出来,与原文第二句合在一起,译为一句。这样既不影响原文表达的内容,同时又突出了原文作者想要对比春景和秋景的意图。

7. 此句和上段的处理相似。"叶落,草枯"提前至第一句,起到了解释说明的作用,语义更加紧凑,也更符合汉语的表达习惯。

8. 此句并不复杂,但若译得过实,难免会影响原文呈现的美感。译者在此充分利用汉语意合的特点,用四字词分别将薄雾、蓝天、暖阳翻译出来,使译文很有画面感,忠实地再现了原文的美景,传递出金秋的意蕴。

9. 此段主要描绘动物为过冬做准备。此句是一个简单句,译者在"for weeks"前增加了"忙活"二字,与前面的 harvesting 和 stowing 两个动作并列起来,以强调动物为过冬所做的准备。

(译注/唐毅)

Singing, Each to Each
你吟我唱

By *Joanna Leyland*
文/乔安娜·莱兰 译/唐毅

译者按：乔安娜·莱兰是一个擅长利用希腊罗马神话中的题材进行创作的作家。本文中海上航行时歌声与男性的故事很有可能就是借鉴了希腊神话中女妖塞壬的故事。本文的特点是景物描写细致入微，感情表达十分充沛。此外本文的背景不详，给译者理解原文会造成一定困难，翻译时在理解上应多下功夫。此外，译者还可以利用汉语意合的特点，将原文中的连接成分省略不译，使译文更加流畅自然。

Dawn is best, when sight joins sound. First, the whisper of waves shows a glimmer, a sheen, becoming a whiteness that edges the sand; then the rocks sigh and gently free their forms from the surrounding dark; the air starts to quiver and murmur with light; and the blur of a bird sounds a single envious trill[1].

We are there, we are ready. We greet the day and the dawn, feeling the hushed heartbeat of the world gathering strength for the effort to come. And then we sing. Perhaps one of us will

黎明时分，美景和自然之声在此刻交汇，这是最美的时刻。起初，海浪呢喃低语，晶莹闪烁的浪花为沙滩缀上一道白边；渐渐地，礁石轻叹着，在周围的一片黑暗中一点点显露出轮廓；空气开始微微颤动，和着光一起喃喃低语；还有孤鸟那一声啁啾，若隐若现，鸣声轻颤，惹人艳羡。

我们就在那里，等待黎明。我们迎接黎明，迎来白昼，感受这世界沉静的心跳，它在为新一天的辛劳积蓄力量。我们禁不住歌唱起来。也许有人会找到一首歌

find a fragment of refrain, some old golden song belonging to legend that has always existed and only needs finding again, and we take it, caress it, give it wings and send it phoenix-like away[2].

Evening has its time too though. Then mellowness deepens to dusk; the waves whisper of rest; stars gently chime; the moon has a deeper note[3]. Sound becomes scent, spicy thyme yielding to fragrance of fern, sun-warmed rocks to coolness of earth. And our song, our celebration, changes in tone.

It must be the celebration, the feeling of joy that maddens them. When they hear it, they feel excluded, futile, their heroics reduced to posturing, their words exposed as senseless noise, and … they try to reach it[4]. They beat their way through the waves, while we watch and sing and will not help; we suspect it is not joy but our particular joy they want to reach and conquer. Perhaps they want what we found long ago.

Of course they fail, and of course the stories start, and the fear and the hatred and the hard words, so that truth is made mute in a babble of lies[5]. Sometimes we sing of that as well, but never willingly, never with pleasure, even though we know the song must include all things. No joy can exist without sorrow, and no song without silence either[6].

There was one man who heard and understood— now so far in the past we wonder

的副歌片段，那是一首已成传奇的古老金曲，始终存于世间，只待重新发现。我们找到它，呵护它，予其双翼，令其凤凰涅槃般重生。

然而，黄昏的美景也很动人。彼时，明亮的天色渐渐昏黄；海浪低吟，繁星轻和，月儿低吟。一片静寂中芳香弥漫，蕨类植物的芳香将辛辣的百里香香味掩盖，被阳光晒热的礁石跟随大地逐渐冷却。我们的歌声，我们的欢庆啊，开始变调。

一定是这欢庆、这喜悦的感觉使他们抓狂。耳听狂欢之乐，却不能身在其中，多么沮丧、多么徒劳啊！因为在这歌声的狂欢之中，他们的英雄壮举不过是装腔作势，他们的豪言壮语只是莫名的噪音而已……可是，他们想要加入这狂欢。看着他们破浪前行，我们却袖手旁观，继续欢歌。因为我们怀疑，他们想要得到并征服的不是欢乐本身，而是我们的欢乐。也许他们想要的正是我们早已拥有的。

当然他们没有找到。于是开始有了各种杜撰的故事，恐惧之声、憎恨之语、刺耳之言不绝于耳，因而真理在一大堆谎言中哑然失语。有时，我们也歌颂谎言，纵然不情不愿，毫无乐趣可言。即使我们知道，那首歌必定包容万物。没有悲伤，何来快乐；没有静默，何来歌声？

有个男人听懂了我们的歌声，但已经过去了太久，我们怀疑这是不是一个梦。

if we dreamed him. The ship passed, sleek and swift in the water, the sailors bent double over their oars as though in agony, their faces ugly with fear and loathing. We knew they could not hear us: they labored and strained and did not even look, did not try and dash their lives away.

We watched and sang and the ship became our song[7]. And then that one man—he had heard the tales no doubt and made provision, bound as he was to the mast—suddenly listened. He struggled and shouted to be freed, and then suddenly listened, listened and smiled.

The ship went its way, skimming over the waves in a tumult of foam, our song now urging it on.

船儿在海水中飞快地滑过,水手们使劲地划桨,弓着的身子似乎痛苦不堪,脸部因恐惧和厌恶变得甚是难看。我们知道,他们听不见我们的歌声:他们拼命划呀,划呀,甚至都没抬头看一眼,他们压根就没想过虚度生命。

我们注视着,歌唱着,船儿上歌声飞扬。然后有个男人——无疑他曾听过那些传说,也有所准备。尽管他被绑在桅杆上,在那里挣扎、叫嚷放开他,却突然聆听起来。听着听着,他笑了起来。

船儿在泡沫汹涌的海中破浪疾行。我们的歌啊,开始为它壮行。

注释:

1. 在此段落中,作者采用了拟人的手法,海浪、礁石、空气似乎都有生命,在黎明时分呢喃低语。翻译时,应注意将此修辞手法表现出来。此外最后一个分句看似简单,其实不然。译者将 blur, single, envious, trill 分别拆分出来翻译,使译文不受原文结构束缚,形成汉语典型的流水句式,既达意又地道。

2. 原句是一个较长的复合句,里面包含一个定语从句。翻译时,译者将定语从句拆分出来,以避免定语从句过长,造成"的的不休"的情况。

3. 原文句式统一整齐(主语+谓语),表达简洁。译文需注意保留原文的表达风格。译者采用汉语常见的主谓结构来对应原文的结构,并使用四字词的主谓结构,完美再现了原文的句式结构和语义表达。

4. 译者根据上下文,做了适当的增补,加上了"因为在这歌声的狂欢之中",使"他们的英雄壮举不过是装腔作势,他们的豪言壮语只是莫名的噪音而已……"的语境更加明确,让读者一目了然。

5. 此句中的两个 of course,含义其实是不一样的,翻译时应该注意体会含义的差别。

译者分别译为"当然""于是"进行准确表达。

6. 原句句式对仗工整,采用了"No...without"这种双重否定的结构来表达肯定的意义。译文为了表达出这种肯定的含义,采用反问的语气,"没有……,何来……"完全再现了原文的句式和意义表达,末尾将原文的句号改为问号,既符合汉语表达习惯,又使语气更加强烈,情感表达更加充分。

7. 此分句的理解对汉语读者有些困难。从字面意思上来讲,似乎是"船儿变成了我们的歌声"。汉语显然不会这样表达。其实再想一想,作者想要表达的意思就是"船上到处都是歌声",因此我们可以用"船儿上歌声飞扬"这样地道的汉语来表达。

(译注/唐毅)

First Snow
初　雪

By *Gilean Douglas*

文/吉利亚恩·道格拉斯　　译/唐毅

译者按： 吉利亚恩·道格拉斯(1900—1993)，记者、历史学家、女性主义者及自然主义作家。作为一名热爱自然，热爱写作的女性，她把对自然的热爱融入写作中，因此她写作的主题通常都与自然有关。本文即作者对冬日雪景的描绘。作者观察细致，触角敏锐，文字细腻、文章优美动人。笔触所及，表现出了美丽的大自然和作者对自然的深爱，呈现出诗一般的浓情。翻译时，应注意保持本文这种诗意的基本特征，注意突出散文的描写性和诗歌的表现性。

One evening I look out the window of my secluded cabin, and there are soft languid flakes falling in the golden lamplight[1]. They fall all night, while the voice of the Teal River becomes more and more hushed and the noises of the forest die away. By dawn, the whole world of stream and wood and mountain has been kindled to a white flame of beauty[2].

I go out in the early morning and there is such silence that even breath is a profanation. The mountain to the north has a steel-blue light

一天傍晚，从僻静的小木屋向窗外望去，在金黄色的灯光下，只见片片轻柔的雪花慵懒地飘落下来。梯尔河的水流越来越沉静，森林中的声音渐渐消失殆尽，雪却落了整整一夜。黎明时分，溪流、树林、山峦，早已是银装素裹，熠熠生辉，好一个美丽的世界！

早起，步出户外。周围寂静无声，似乎连呼吸声都会亵渎此时的寂静。北边，山峦笼罩在一片铁青色中；西边，天空依

on it, and to the west the sky still holds something of the darkness of the night. To the east and the south a faint pink is spreading[3]. I look up and see the morning star keeping white[4] watch over a white world.

Soon the whole sky is azure and flamingo. Every branch of every tree is weighted with cold and stillness; every fallen log is overlaid with silver. The wild berry bushes have puffballs of jeweler's cotton here and there along their branches, and the stark roots of hemlocks and cedars have become grottoes of quartz and chrysolite.

After heavy snowfalls, it is the evergreens that are the loveliest, with their great white branches weighted down until they are almost parallel with the trunks. They seem like giant birds with their wings folded against the cold[5].

But after a light fall[6], it is the deciduous trees that are the most beautiful. They are so fragile, so ethereal, that it seems even the sound of the rivers might shatter them as they appear to drift like crystal smoke along the banks. The bushes are silver filigree, so light, so much on tiptoe in this enchanted world. Even the slightest breeze sends the snow shimmering down from them, leaving the branches brown and bare and rather pitiful.

The sky is clear blue now and the sun has flung diamonds down on meadow and bank and wood. Beauty, the virgin, walks here quietly,

稀残留着些许朦胧的夜色；东边和南边的天空中，淡淡的粉红正在一点一点地蔓延。抬头仰望，明亮的启明星还注视着这个白茫茫的世界。

不一会，湛蓝和火红两种色彩在空中交织。颗颗树木、条条树枝上积满了白雪，沉甸甸的，显得冰冷静谧；每一根倒伏的木头都覆满了银白色的雪。灌木丛中，野浆果的枝条上到处是朵朵雪绒球，轻柔蓬松得好似马勃菌朵。铁杉和雪松光秃秃的树根里满是石英石和橄榄石。

几场暴雪过后，最可爱的要数冬青树了。它们那巨大的白色枝桠被雪压得几乎和树干平行，看起来就像蜷缩着翅膀以御严寒的大鸟。

而小雪过后，最美的还是那些落叶树了。它们就像晶莹的尘烟飘散在河流两岸，多么脆弱，多么缥缈，似乎潺潺的水声都会将它们震碎。灌木丛好似一根根银丝，那么轻盈、那么小心地踮着脚尖伫立在这个迷人的世界。即使最轻柔的微风也会吹得树上的白雪一闪一闪地飘落，剩下褐色的树枝，光秃秃的，惹人怜爱。

此刻，天空清澈湛蓝。太阳撒下千万颗宝石，落在草地上，落在河岸边，落在树林里。美神处子，在这里轻轻地、轻轻地

quietly. Her feet make no sound and not sign upon the immaculate snow. The silence is dense and deep. Even the squirrels have stopped their ribald chattering. And faint snowbird whisperings seem to emphasize the stillness.

  Night comes, and the silence holds. There is a feeling about this season that is in no other—a sense of snugness, security and solitude. It is good to be out in the bracing cold, which clears the mind and invigorates the heart. Blanket, fire is a first-rate companion. The coffee is full-bodied and fragrant; shadows dance on the walls and the world outside my windows is very still. I am more than content to begin and end a day like this amid all the calm clarity of wintered earth.

  Outside the moon is high with a dark-blue sky behind it and with mountains, plains and forests of silver lying below. The trees, the bushes and the tall ferns are carved with alabaster. The river runs like quick silver between the porcelain of its banks.

  Earth and heavens glitter, and the sword-fern clumps are diamond sunbursts pinned to the silver-sequined ground. But it is all in silence. There are shadows from the stars. They are white, sharp lights in the midnight blue sky and appear literally to spark with coldness[7]. I feel as though I can see every star in the universe.

  It seems impossible for one human heart to contain all this loveliness without breaking.

漫步。在洁白无瑕的雪地上,她脚步无声,踏雪无痕。世界处于深深的静谧之中,连松鼠也停止了吱吱的鼓噪。而那雪鸟若有若无的低鸣之声,衬托得四周更加静谧。

  夜晚来临,依然是万籁俱寂。安适惬意和清净独处的感觉非此季节莫属。在屋外的雪地里甚感惬意,这清新的寒意,让人头脑清醒,精神振奋。此时毛毯、炉火是最佳的伴侣,咖啡浓郁香醇。墙上清影弄舞。而窗外的世界却是那般静寂。在这宁静清澈的冬日,迎来光阴,送走时光,自是好生欢喜。

  屋外,深蓝色的夜空中,月儿高悬,其下是银色的山峦、平川和森林。树木、灌丛,还有那高高的蕨类植物好似冰雕玉砌。宛如白皙瓷胎的河岸之间,梯尔河水似水银般流淌。

  天地闪亮,一簇簇剑蕨类植物好似亮闪闪的圆形钻石胸针,别在银光闪烁的大地上。然而,世界依然一片沉寂。在午夜深蓝的天空下,星星投下的点点白影似耀眼的星灯,闪烁着寒光。似乎,能看见宇宙中的每一颗星星。

  世间美景可爱如斯,一颗凡人之心何能溢满而不裂?心知指尖轻触,美景即

Perhaps the ache that is in mine comes from the knowledge that all this beauty is so ephemeral, that it will be gone almost before I have done more than touch it with my fingertips.

逝，自是心痛不已。

▶▶ 注释：

1. 此文从第一人称视角写成，译者认为在此文中无需将人称翻译出来。这样处理的好处在于：首先不会影响文章意思的表达，其次可以更好地将读者的注意力集中在作者对美景的描述中。下文对人称也做了同样的处理。

2. 原文是一个简单的被动语态的句子，如果不做拆分，意思虽然容易表达完整，但散文诗一样的韵味却会失去。在此，译者采用分拆的方法，将此句子拆分为2个句子，更好地表达出原文的意思。

3. 原文是描述东南西北四面的美景，是两个单独的句子。译者根据汉语的特点，将其合并为一个句子，分句之间用分号隔开。这样的处理完整地保留了原文的表达结构，也更符合汉语的表达习惯。

4. 句子中的启明星就是金星，是日出和日落时分出现在天空的最亮的星星。keeping white watch 中的 white 是属于转移修饰词，它是用来修饰 morning star 的。日出时分的启明星最亮，相比四周残留的朦胧夜色，闪亮的星星肉眼可见的颜色就是白色，故而译者将其翻译为"明亮的"。

5. 此段做了断句和合句的处理。第一句做了断句处理，将 with their great white branches weighted down until they are almost parallel with the trunks 从句中断开，合并到段落的第二句中，使译文表达的意思更加紧密。

6. light fall 是相对于上一段讲了 heavy fall（大雪）之后，开始讲小雪降落之后的美景。此处的 light 容易误解为阳光。

7. 此处将原文的两个句子合并成了一个句子翻译。因为原文第二句的 they 就是指上一句的 shadows，合并后的句子的意思表达自然、流畅，两个句子联系更加紧密。

（译注／唐毅）

Appetite
欲　望

By *Laurie Lee*

文/劳里·李　译/唐毅

译者按：劳里·李（1914—1997）是一位英国诗人、剧作家、自传作家和儿童小说作家。作者从对食物的欲望入手，表现他对人类欲望这一永恒主题的思考。本文短小精悍、结构紧凑。无论以自己孩童时代的还是古代社会的经历，对食物的渴望到所有人类的欲望，作者都紧紧围绕主题进行论述，主题十分鲜明，也很有说服力。文章的标题"appetite"原指"胃口"。但因为文章本身是从人对食物的欲望（即胃口）拓展到人类的其他欲望进行讨论，所以还是译为"欲望"更准确，更能涵盖文章讨论的内容。

One of the major pleasures in life is appetite, and one of our major duties should be to preserve it. Appetite is the keenness of living; it is one of the senses that tells you that you are still curious to exist, that you still have an edge on your longings and want to bite into the world and taste its multitudinous flavors and juices[1].

By appetite, of course, I don't mean just the lust for food, but any condition of

人生的一大乐趣就是欲望，保持欲望不失是我们的主要责任之一。欲望是对生活的渴望；欲望是我们的七情六欲之一，表明你对生活依然好奇，你还有热切的希望，你想品味这个世界，品味它的万千风味和玉液琼浆。

当然欲望并非只是对食物的渴望，而是那种未能如愿的状况，是那种热血

unsatisfied desire, any burning in the blood that proves you want more than you've got, and that you haven't yet used up your life². Wilde said he felt sorry for those who never got their heart's desire, but sorrier still for those who did. I got mine once only, and it nearly killed me, and I've always preferred wanting to having since.

  For appetite, to me, is this state of wanting, which keeps one's expectations alive. I remember learning the lesson long ago as a child, when treats and orgies were few, and when I discovered that the greatest pitch of happiness was not in actually eating a toffee but in gazing at it beforehand. True, the first bite was delicious, but once the toffee was gone one was left with nothing, neither toffee nor lust. Besides, the whole toffeeness³ of toffees was imperceptibly diminished by the gross act of having eaten it. No, the best was in wanting it, in sitting and looking at it, when one tasted an inexhaustible treasure-house of flavors.

  So, for me, one of the keenest pleasures of appetite remains in the wanting, not the satisfaction. In wanting a peach, or a whisky, or a particular texture or sound, or to be with a particular friend. For in this condition, of course, I know that the object of desire is always at its most flawlessly perfect. Which is why I would carry the preservation of appetite to the extent of deliberate fasting, simply because I

沸腾的感觉。这感觉说明你因渴望拥有更多,感觉未尽享生活而焦灼。王尔德曾经说过,他同情那些从来未能如愿之人,但他更同情那些事事如愿之人。曾经有一次我实现了愿望,可却让我难过得要死。从那以后,我总是更乐于向往而非拥有。

  对我来说,欲望便是这样一种向往的状态,它让人时刻有所期待。记得早在孩提时代我就懂得这个道理。小时候很少受人款待,也没有机会大吃大喝,那时我就发现最大的快乐并不是吃太妃糖,而是在吃之前目不转睛地盯着它看的时候。事实也是如此。确实,咬第一口时,甜美无比,但吃完之后,便什么也没有了。太妃糖没了,吃糖的欲望也随之而去。更糟的是,因为囫囵吞枣,太妃糖的甜美滋味也在不知不觉中消减了。没错,当你品尝一屋子享用不尽的各种美味之时,最美好的感觉是在坐而视之、内心向往之时。

  因此我认为,欲望的最大欢愉在于有所向往,而非得偿所愿。比如想吃一个蜜桃,想喝一杯威士忌,想要一种特别的质感或一首好曲,或是想和某位好友做伴。我知道在此心境下,心之所想自是完美无瑕。为此,为了保持食欲我甚至故意禁食,只因食欲美好不可失去,它弥足珍贵,岂可因暴饮暴食而使其麻木?

think that appetite is too good to lose, too precious to be bludgeoned into insensibility by satiation and over-doing it[4].

For that matter, I don't really want three square meals a day—I want one huge, delicious, orgiastic, table-groaning blow-out, say every four days[5], and then not be too sure where the next one is coming from. A day of fasting is not for me just a puritanical device for denying oneself a pleasure, but rather a way of anticipating a rare moment of supreme indulgence.

Fasting is an act of homage to the majesty of appetite. So I think we should arrange to give up our pleasures regularly—our food, our friends, our lovers—in order to preserve their intensity, and the moment of coming back to them. For this is the moment that renews and refreshes both oneself and the thing one loves. Sailors and travelers enjoyed this once, and so did hunters, I suppose. Part of the weariness of modern life may be that we live too much on top of each other[6], and are entertained and fed too regularly. Once we were separated by hunger both from our food and families, and then we learned to value both[7]. The men went off hunting, and the dogs went with them; the women and children waved goodbye. The cave was empty of men for days on end; nobody ate, or knew what to do. The women crouched by the fire, the wet smoke[8] in their eyes; the

正因如此，我并不想一日三餐顿顿丰盛可口——而是想每隔几天享用一餐美味。比如每隔几天备一桌美味佳肴，享用一顿饕餮盛宴，而饱餐之后又不太清楚下一顿会在哪里。禁食一日于我而言并非是清教徒式的节欲，而是以此期待那难得的尽情放纵享受的一刻。

禁食是为了向神圣欲望致敬。因此我认为应该不时刻意放弃一些欢愉——如美食、好友、恋人——以保持欢愉的深刻感受和欢愉失而复得的美妙时刻。因为这种时刻，能让人重新焕发精神，能让所爱之物焕然一新。水手、旅人都曾体会这样的时刻，我想猎人也不例外。我们对现代生活感到厌倦，部分原因或许就是我们平时交往太过密切，娱乐、饱食太过规律。我们曾经因为没有食物而饥饿难忍，曾经和家人被迫分离，于是我们才学会珍惜。那时，男人带着狗出门打猎，妻儿与之挥手告别。山洞里一连数天都不见男人的身影；没人吃饭，大伙都不知所措。妇女蹲在火堆边，被烟熏得两眼是泪，孩子哭号着，人人饥肠辘辘。直到一天晚上，忽听山上传来人的叫喊和犬吠声，男人们满载肉食而归。这是盛大的

children wailed; everybody was hungry. Then one night there were shouts and the barking of dogs from the hills, and the men came back loaded with meat. This was the great reunion, and everybody gorged themselves silly, and appetite came into its own; the long-awaited meal became a feast to remember and an almost sacred celebration of life. Now we go off to the office and come home in the evenings to cheap chicken and frozen peas. Very nice, but too much of it, too easy and regular, served up without effort or wanting[9]. We eat, we are lucky, our faces are shining with fat, but we don't know the pleasure of being hungry any more.

Too much of anything—too much music, entertainment, happy snacks, or time spent with one's friends—creates a kind of impotence of living by which one can no longer hear, or taste, or see, or love, or remember[10]. Life is short and precious, and appetite is one of its guardians, and loss of appetite is a sort of death. So if we are to enjoy this short life we should respect the divinity of appetite, and keep it eager and not too much blunted.

It is a long time now since I knew that acute moment of bliss that comes from putting parched lips to a cup of cold water. The springs are still there to be enjoyed—all one needs is the original thirst.

团圆,每个人都食欲大开,狼吞虎咽,大快朵颐。连日来翘首以盼的大餐成了难忘的盛筵,几乎成了人生的庆典。而如今,我们白天上班,晚上回家,吃的却是廉价鸡肉和冻豆子。尽管也不错,但就是食物太过丰裕,唾手可得,按时按点,无须费力,也无须期盼就能吃到。结果我们吃得油光满面。幸运的是我们没有挨饿,但我们却再也体会不到饥饿的快感了。

任何事物太多——如音乐听得太多、娱乐过度、可口的小吃太多,或和朋友相处太久等等——人都会变得对生活无能为力。它使人悦耳之乐不闻,佳肴珍馐无味,对美妙爱情无感,对美好的时光失忆。生命短暂宝贵,需要欲望来守护,失去欲望无异于生命死亡。因此,若要享受这美好短暂的人生,就应尊重神圣的欲望,要让它热烈持久而不会变得太迟钝。

焦渴的双唇够到一杯清凉之水那一瞬间的幸福,我早已久违。甘泉常有,待人以尝,而我们需要的仅是那最原始的渴望罢了。

注释:

1. 此句较长。一般对于较长的句子,我们都可以通过拆分进行断句,这样就可以避免译文生硬。此句通过拆分,将原句拆分为汉语的五个流水句,既达意又流畅。此外,句中的两个词语:flavors 和 juices 似不宜翻译为"酸甜苦辣、人生百味"。虽然单词本身确实包含了这样的含义,但从文章表达的观点来看,人的欲望是对自身有利、美好的事物,而非不好的事物,故译为"万千风味和玉液琼浆"。

2. 此句中的定语从句拆分出来,单独成句,使表达更清楚,句子更流畅。

3. toffeeness 一词为作者所造,意指太妃糖的美味。

4. 原句为陈述句,翻译时将其改为反问句,能更好地保留原文的意思和语气。

5. 根据上下文,可以看出作者并非彻底绝食,而是想通过适当的节食来增加对美味佳肴的感知。所以翻译时,适当地通过增词手法,增加"顿顿丰盛可口"使语义更加准确、完整。此外,"every four days"中的数词 four 是虚指,不用照实译出。

6. 此句中"on top of each other"是"close, intimate"之意,所以翻译时需做适当的词义引申进行处理,故译为"(交往太过)密切"。

7. 译文重复"曾经"一词,是为了与后面讲述的古代故事更加契合。古代故事是为了例证此句中所表达的意思,即人们因为饥饿,缺乏食物,所以男人出去打猎,妇孺婴幼留守家中,饱受饥饿折磨,忍受家人分开的痛苦。

8. 此处指因烟熏而使眼睛流泪。

9. 严格地讲,这个句子不是完整的句子。原文有表达让步状语之意,译文中需将此翻译出来,更符合汉语习惯,故译文加上"尽管"一词。此外,为了使译文表达的语义更加紧凑,可以对形容词的词序略做一点调整。

10. 原文很简洁,翻译时需要将原文省略的宾语补充出来,同时也要保持原文几个并列谓语所表达出来的句式。因此译文在处理这几个并列谓语的时候,尽量采用对仗工整的句式。

(译注/唐毅)

Lord Chesterfield's Letter to His Son
切斯费尔德勋爵的《致子书》

By *Philip Dormer Stanhope*
文/菲利普·多默·斯坦诺普 译/唐毅

译者按：菲利普·多默·斯坦诺普(1694—1773)系英国政治家和文学家。他与其子菲利普·斯坦诺普之间有长达三十余年的通信，内容主要涵盖地理、历史，文学经典以及政治、外交等。本文是切斯费尔德勋爵写给当时年仅七岁的儿子的信，信中表达了父亲对儿子的拳拳关爱之心，并提出了交友的一些建议。文末表达了对儿子的监督之意，不惜用好友监督作为威胁，实乃用心良苦。

DEAR BOY: People of your age have, commonly, an unguarded frankness about them; which makes them the easy prey and bubbles[1] of the artful and the experienced; they look upon every knave or fool, who tells them that he is their friend, to be really so; and pay that profession of simulated friendship, with an indiscreet and unbounded confidence, always to their loss, often to their ruin.

Beware, therefore, now that you are coming into the world, of these preferred friendships. Receive them with great civility,

亲爱的儿子：年轻人在你这样的年纪，通常对人非常坦率，毫无防备之心，这使他们很容易成为那些狡猾老练之徒的猎物或炫耀的谈资；那些流氓、莽汉说是他们的朋友，他们就信以为真，于是对这种虚假友情的告白毫无戒备、完全信任，最后总是吃亏，还常常毁了自己。

因此，来到这个世界，你就应该警惕此类被人莫名偏爱的友情。礼貌接受，但完全不要轻信；报以感谢，但不与他们亲

Lord Chesterfield's Letter to His Son

but with great, incredulity too; and pay them with compliments, but not with confidence[2]. Do not let your vanity and self-love make you suppose that people become your friends at first sight, or even upon a short acquaintance.

  Real friendship is a slow grower and never thrives unless engrafted upon a stock of known and reciprocal merit[3]. There is another kind of nominal friendship among young people, which is warm for the time, but by good luck, of short duration. This friendship is hastily produced, by their being accidentally thrown together, and pursuing the course of riot and debauchery. A fine friendship, truly; and well cemented by drunkenness and lewdness. It should rather be called a conspiracy against morals and good manners, and *be* punished as such by the civil magistrate[4]. However, they have the impudence and folly to call this confederacy a friendship. They lend one another money, for bad purposes; they engage in quarrels, offensive and defensive for their accomplices; they tell one another all they know, and often more too, when, of a sudden, some accident disperses them, and they think no more of each other, unless it be to betray and laugh, at their imprudent confidence.

  Remember to make a great difference between companions and friends; for a very complaisant and agreeable companion may, and often does, prove a very improper and a very

近。倘若以为初次见面或相识不久,别人就会成为你的朋友,这不过是你自己的虚荣和自恋作祟罢了。

  真正的友谊是慢慢生长起来的,只有彼此了解、互有美德,友谊之树才会枝繁叶茂。年轻人之间还有一种名不符实的友谊,热络一时,但幸好并不长久。他们偶然相逢,因聚众闹事、寻欢作乐而匆匆结缘成为朋友。这种因酒色而更加牢固的"美好"友谊,其实就是沆瀣一气。这种"友谊"更应被称作对道德和礼仪的"违背",当受地方官惩戒。可他们还将此种乌合之盟称作友谊,真是厚颜无耻、愚蠢至极! 此等乌合之众相互借钱干坏事;为同伙吵架斗殴;彼此之间无所隐瞒,甚至信口开河。而若突遇意外之事,众人就如鸟兽散去,从此相忘于江湖,非是背叛或嘲笑对方鲁莽轻信而不再提起。

  记得要分清同伴和朋友的区别。通常,一个恭顺唯诺的同伴并不合适,也很危险。人们常常根据你的朋友来评价你本人,这样做并非没有道理。有句西班牙

dangerous friend. People will, in a great degree, and not without reason, form their opinion of you, upon that which they have of your friends; and there is a Spanish proverb, which says very justly, TELL ME WHO YOU LIVE WITH AND I WILL TELL YOU WHO YOU ARE.

One may fairly[5] suppose, that the man who makes a knave or a fool his friend, has something very bad to do or to conceal. But, at the same time that you carefully decline the friendship of knaves and fools, if it can be called friendship, there is no occasion to make either of them your enemies, wantonly and unprovoked; for they are numerous bodies, and I, would rather choose a secure neutrality, than alliance, or war with either of them.

You may be a declared[6] enemy to their vices and follies, without being marked out by them as a personal one. Their enmity is the next dangerous thing to their friendship. Have a real reserve with almost everybody; and have a seeming reserve with almost nobody; for it is very disagreeable to seem reserved, and very dangerous not to be so. Few people find the true medium; many are ridiculously mysterious and reserved upon trifles; and many imprudently communicative of all they know.

The next thing to the choice of your friends, is the choice of your company. Endeavor, as much as you can, to keep company with people above you; there you

谚语说得好：告诉我你和谁在一起，我就知道你是什么样的人。

也许有人会这样想，一个人与流氓、莽汉之徒为友，不是要干坏事，就是有坏事相瞒。这样想，并不为过。可是，你应该谨慎地谢绝流氓、莽汉的友谊（如果这也可称作友谊的话），但无论如何，不可任性或无端与他们为敌。因为他们人数众多。我宁愿选择折中处理，既不与其为友，也不与其为敌，此乃安全无虞之道。

即便你与他们毫无私怨，他们也可能因你会妨碍其为非作歹而公然视你为敌。这种敌意的害处仅次于与其为友。对任何人你内心都要真正有所保留，但对任何人你看上去都要显得坦率；因为表面看起来矜持内敛，不能合群，但事事袒露无遗，又非常危险。少有人能真正把握好这个尺度。许多人在无关紧要之小事上显得神秘莫测，真是荒谬可笑；而不少人知无不言，也绝非谨慎之举。

择友之外，最重要的莫过于选择同伴了。你要尽可能结交那些比自己优秀的人，因为近朱者赤，近墨者黑；如前所说，人以类聚也。

rise, as much as you sink with people below you; for (as I have mentioned before) you are whatever the company you keep is.

Do not mistake, when I say company above you, and think that I mean with regard to, their birth: that is the least consideration; but I mean with regard to their merit, and the light in which the world considers them.

There are two sorts of good company; one, which is called the beau monde, and consists of the people who have the lead in courts, and in the gay parts of life; the other consists of those who are distinguished by some peculiar merit, or who excel in some particular and valuable art or science. For my own part, I used to think myself in company as, much above me, when I was with Mr. Addison[7] and Mr. Pope[8], as if I had been with all the princes in Europe. What I mean by low company, which should by all means be avoided, is the company of those, who, absolutely insignificant and contemptible in themselves, think they are honored by being in your company: and who flatter vice and every folly you have, in order to engage you to converse with them[9]. The pride of being the first of the company is but too common: but it is very silly and very prejudicial. Nothing in the world lets down a character quicker than that wrong turn.

You may possibly ask me, whether a man has it always in his power to get the best

所谓比你优秀之同伴,不要误以为是那些出身家世比你好的人。此乃最无须考虑之事。我说的优秀,是指他们身上的美德以及世人对他们的评价更胜于你。

世上有两种良伴。一种是上流社会之人,他们是宫廷的主角,引领时尚生活之人;另一种是因特殊的美德而受人尊敬,或是某一珍贵的、特殊的艺术或科学领域的杰出人士。以我个人来说,过去一直与艾迪生和蒲柏为伴,在我看来这就是与优秀之人为伴。与他们交往,如同和欧洲的王公贵族结交一样。所谓不良之伴是指那些本身卑鄙猥琐,却以与你为伴而荣之人。还有那些极尽谄媚之人,为了与你攀谈,你的恶习和你干的每件蠢事,他们都会阿谀奉承。你必须想方设法避免与其交往。与第一类人做伴而感到骄傲,是人之常情,但绝非聪明之举,反而贻害自己。世上没有什么比走错方向更容易让人遭遇挫折了。

也许你会问,一个人是否总是能结交到最优秀的同伴?如何才能结交到最优

company? And how? I say, Yes, he has, by deserving it; providing he is but in circumstances which enable him to appear upon the footing of a gentleman. Merit and good-breeding will make their way everywhere. Knowledge will introduce him, and good-breeding will endear him to the best companies: for, as I have often told you, politeness and good-breeding are absolutely necessary to adorn any, or all other good qualities or talents. Without them, no knowledge, no perfection whatever, is seen in its best light. The scholar, without good-breeding, is a pedant; the philosopher, a cynic; the soldier, a brute; and every man disagreeable[10].

I long to hear, from my several correspondents at Leipsig, of your arrival there, and what impression you make on them at first; for I have Arguses[11], with an hundred eyes each, who will watch you narrowly, and relate to me faithfully. My accounts will certainly be true; it depends upon you, entirely, of what kind they shall be. Adieu.

秀的同伴？我的回答是肯定的，办法是让自己成为一个绅士，配得上他们，值得让他们与你为伴。在这世上，美德和良好的教养畅行无阻。知识助他有机会结识优秀之人，良好的教养令他受其喜爱。正如我常常告诉你的，无论何人，礼貌和教养都能为他的其他任何优秀品质和才能增色添魅。否则，任何知识、任何成就都会黯然失色。没有教养的学者，只是学究而已；没有教养的哲人，只是尖酸刻薄之徒；没有教养的士兵，不过一介屠夫。一个人没有教养，总是令人讨厌。

我盼望着在莱比锡的好友，告诉我你是否平安抵达，谈谈他们对你的第一印象。我在那里的友人，就像希腊神话里的阿耳戈斯，个个都有百眼在身。他们会密切关注你，并将你的一举一动如实告诉我。我在信里将会忠实地记下你在那里的一切，当然信里的内容，完全取决于你的表现。再见。

▶ 注释：

1. bubble 在此是指耗费精力用来装点炫耀的人或事，故译为用以"炫耀的谈资"。

2. 原文是祈使句后接两个介词短语，后面一个介词短语意思有所转折。翻译时应注意保持原文的句式和语气，因此译为"……，但不……"

3. 作者用树的生长来比喻友谊的发展，用了 thrives, engrafted 等词，所以翻译时应尽量将修辞手法表达出来，故译者翻译为"友谊之树才会枝繁叶茂"。

4. 此句宜采用分拆的方法,将 against morals and good manners 拆出,合并到后面一个分句进行翻译。分拆避免了修饰成分较长而形成欧化句式的现象。

5. 此句将副词 fairly 拆出,单独成句,使译文表达更地道、更流畅。

6. declared 一词原做形容词,翻译时可将其改变词性,译为副词"公然地",这样句子表达更流畅一些。

7. 约瑟夫·艾迪生(1672—1719):英国散文家、诗人、剧作家、政治家。

8. 亚历山大·蒲柏(1688—1744):英国诗人、文学评论家。

9. 原句很长,句子成分复杂,含有主语从句、定语从句等,需做断句分拆处理。注意分拆应按照不同的语义进行,才能使句子的意思表达明确。同时,可将句子开头部分的 which should by all means be avoided 调整到最后,即先将不良之伴的种种劣性列举出来,然后总结不应与此类人交往。这样语序调整的好处在于比较符合汉语表达习惯。

10. 原文使用了省略句,语言简洁,排列工整。在译文中,需要将省略的部分增补出来,同时也要尽量保留原文的句式,所以译者采用"没有……,只是(不过)……"这样的句式,将几个分句并列起来。

11. 阿耳戈斯系希腊神话里的百眼怪兽。

(译注/唐毅)

On Doors
门 之 思

By *Christopher Darlington Morley*
文/克里斯托夫·达林顿·莫利　译/唐毅

译者按：克里斯托夫·达林顿·莫利(1890—1957)系美国作家。他是一位多产作家,一生创作了百余部小说和大量的散文、诗歌、戏剧等作品。莫利的散文诙谐幽默,观点独到,善于观察常人忽略的事物,并从中得到启迪。本篇即是如此。作者从最为平常的开门关门入手,引发对变幻莫测的命运以及人生悲欢离合的思考。

The opening and closing of doors are the most significant action of man's life. What a mystery lies in doors!

No man knows what awaits him when he opens a door. Even the most familiar room, where the clock ticks and the hearth glows red at dusk, may harbor surprises. The plumber may actually have called (while you were out) and fixed that leaking faucet. The cook may have had a fit of the vapors and demanded her passports. The wise man opens his front door with humility and a spirit of acceptance.

人的一生,最有意义的动作莫过于开门和关门。门是多么的神秘啊!

开门时,没有人知道门后等待他的是什么。即使在你最熟悉不过的房间,这个黄昏时刻钟声嘀嗒、炉火熊熊的地方,都可能藏着意想不到之事。(当你不在家时)水管工也许上门,修好了漏水的龙头。厨娘也许会突生忧郁,要求同意她离开。聪明的人总是怀着谦逊和包容之心打开他的大门。

On Doors

Which one of us has not sat in some anteroom and watched the inscrutable panels of a door that was full of meaning? Perhaps you were waiting to apply for a job; perhaps you had some "deal" you were ambitious to put over. You watched the confidential stenographer flit in and out, carelessly turning that mystic portal which, to you, revolved on hinges of fate[1]. And then the young woman said, "Mr. Cranberry will see you now." As you grasped the knob the thought flashed, "when I open this door again, what will have happened?"

There are many kinds of doors. Revolving doors for hotels, shops and public buildings. These are typical of the brisk, bustling ways of modern life. Can you imagine John Milton[2] or William Penn[3] skipping through a revolving doors? Then there are the curious little slatted doors that still swing outside denatured barrooms and extend only from shoulder to knee. There are trapdoors, sliding doors, double doors, stage doors, prison doors, glass doors. But the symbol and mystery of a door resides in its quality of concealment. A glass door is not a door at all, but a window. The meaning of a door is to hide what lies inside; to keep the heart in suspense.

Also, there are many ways of opening doors. There is the cheery push[4] of elbow with which the waiter shoves open the kitchen door when he bears in your tray of supper. There is

有谁不曾坐在某个接待室,盯着神秘莫测、却又意味深长的门上的镶板呢?也许你正在找工作;也许你有一笔渴望达成的"交易"。盯着机要速记员轻快地走进走出,漫不经心地转动那扇神秘之门,于你,那道门上转动的铰链就是你变幻莫测的命运。过了一会,那位年轻女郎说,"克兰贝里先生现在要见你。"于是你抓住门把手,思绪飞快转动,"等我再打开此门时,又会是怎样了呢?"

门有多种。旅馆、商场、公共建筑的旋转门,它们代表活泼、热闹的现代生活方式。你能想象约翰·弥尔顿或者威廉·佩恩匆匆穿过旋转门吗?还有老式酒馆外面那些用板条装饰的奇怪小门,只有膝到肩的高度,酒馆早已改作他用,而小门依然在外面晃来荡去。还有地板门、滑门、双扇门、舞台门、牢门、玻璃门等等。可是门的象征意义和神秘之处在于它的隐藏特性。玻璃门根本算不上门,不过是一扇窗户而已。门的意义在于隐藏门后之物,引人猜想。

同样,开门的方式多种多样。侍者端起餐盘,兴冲冲地用胳膊推开厨房门给你送餐;在沮丧的书商和小贩面前,门也许会在犹疑中打开;穿着制服的男仆缓缓拉

the suspicious and tentative withdrawal of a door before the unhappy book agent or peddler. There is the genteel and carefully modulated recession with which footmen swing wide the oaken barriers of the great[5]. There is the sympathetic and awful silence of the dentist's maid who opens the door into the operating room and, without speaking, implies that the doctor is ready for you. There is the brisk cataclysmic opening of a door when the nurse comes in, very early in the morning—"It's a boy!"

  Doors are the symbols of privacy, of retreat, of the mind's escape into blissful quietude or sad secret struggle. A room without doors is not a room, but a hallway. No matter where he is, a man can make himself at home behind a closed door. The mind works best behind closed doors. Men are not horses to be herded together. Dogs know the meaning and anguish of doors. Have you ever noticed a puppy yearning at a shut portal? It is a symbol of human life.

  The opening of doors is a mystic act: it has in it some flavor of the unknown, some sense of moving into a new moment, a new pattern of the human rigmarole. It includes the highest glimpse of mortal gladness: reunions, reconciliations, the bliss of lovers long parted. Even in sadness, the opening of a door may bring relief: it changes and redistributes human

开橡木制的豪门,彬彬有礼却也小心翼翼;当牙医助理一言不发地打开手术室门时,你明白医生已经等你就医,这时助理的沉默让你既感受到同情,也让你害怕;还有大清早护士走进来,那是哗地一下推门而入,只听她高喊一声:"是个男孩!"

  门象征隐私、退避,象征心灵遁入宁静之至乐或暗自悲伤地挣扎。没有门的房间不是房间,只是一个过道而已。一个人无论身处何处,只要把门一关,就可自由自在。关门之后,心灵最为智慧。人非马,无须被赶至一处,狗也明白门意味着什么,明白门带给它的痛苦。你可曾注意过对着紧闭的房门吠叫的小狗?门是人生的一个象征。

  开门是神秘之举:它既有未知世界的某种味道,又有某种进入新时刻的感觉,让你觉得人生冗常之态有了新的方式。开门那一刹那闪现的是人间最大的快乐:重聚、和解、恋人久别重逢后的喜悦。即使在悲伤之时,开启一扇门也会给人带来安慰,因为它改变并重新分配人内心的力量。而关门则可怕得多,它直白地(直

forces. But the closing of doors is far more terrible. It is a confession of finality. Every door closed brings something to an end. And there are degrees of sadness in the closing of doors. A door slammed is a confession of weakness. A door gently shut is often the most tragic gesture in life. Every one knows the seizure of anguish that comes just after the closing of a door, when the loved one is still near, within sound of voice, and yet already far away[6].

The opening and closing of doors is a part of the stern fluency of life. Life will not stay still and let us alone. We are continually opening doors with hope, closing them with despair. Life lasts not much longer than a pipe of tobacco[7], and destiny knocks us out like the ashes.

The closing of a door is irrevocable. It snaps the packthread of the heart. It is no avail to reopen, to go back. Pinero[8] spoke nonsense when he made Paula Tanqueray say, "The future is only the past entered through another gate." Alas, there is no other gate. When the door is shut, it is shut forever. There is no other entrance to that vanished pulse of time. "The moving finger writes, and having writ"—[9]

There is a certain kind of door-shutting that will come to us all. The kind of door-shutting that is done very quietly, with the sharp click of

接）地宣告这就是结局，因为每一扇关闭的门都意味着一种结束。关门的动作中，或多或少都带着悲伤。"砰"的一声关门，是承认自己的虚弱；轻轻将门关上则是生命中最悲哀的动作，相信每个人都明白关门之后的锥心之痛：那一刻，所爱之人近在咫尺，音容犹在，其实早已撒手人寰。

门之开合是生命执著流动的一部分。生命不会静止停滞，终将离开我们，于是我们总是满怀希望将门开启，却又绝望地把门关上。生命并不比燃尽一斗烟丝长久多少，命运终将打败我们，让我们灰飞烟灭。

生命之门终将关闭，不会再开，牵动心脏的生命之绳随之而断。想要重新打开，再回到过去亦是徒劳。皮内罗借剧中人葆拉·坦克里之口说，"未来只是从另一扇门进入的过去。"这简直是一派胡言，唉，哪里还有另一扇门呢？当这扇门关上，就永远关上了，消失的生命脉动再也没有了别的入口。"指动字成，字成指动。"——

我们每个人终将迎来关门。那是一种悄无声息的关门，唯有门闩咔哒一声落下，打破四周的宁静。那时，真希望他们

the latch to break the stillness. They will think then, one hopes, of our unfulfilled decencies rather than of our pluperfected misdemeanors. Then they will go out and close the door.

只会想到我们未竟的善举,而非我们所行的不端。然后他们自己也会出去,把门关上。

注释:

1. 此句说的是门所代表的是变化多端的命运。

2. 约翰·弥尔顿(1608—1674),英国诗人,因创作 *Paradise Lost* 和 *Paradise Regained* 而闻名于世。

3. 威廉·佩恩(1644—1718),北美殖民地时期英国地产商和哲学家。

4. 译者采用词性转换的方法将此处的 cheer push 转换为副词+动词,更符合汉语表达习惯。

5. 此句虽不复杂,但如果照搬原文结构,读起来不免会结屈聱牙,因此译者采用拆词的手法,将 genteel 和 carefully 分拆出来,单独译出。

6. 关门也意指生命走到尽头。对于"when the loved one is still near, within sound of voice, and yet already far away"这个分句,译者根据上下文做了语义引申,译文表达的意思与原文无异,但更清晰。

7. 作者将生命与一斗烟丝相比,表示生命短暂。因此,译者采用增补的方式,加上"燃尽"二字,使句子意思表达更加清楚。

8. 皮内罗(Sir Arthur Wing Pinero, 1855—1934)系英国剧作家。葆拉·坦克里(Paula Tanqueray)是其创作的戏剧 *The Second Mrs. Tanqueray* 中的女主人公。

9. 此句出自莪默·伽亚谟(波斯诗人)写的《鲁拜集》第71首。译文采用郭沫若先生的译文:"指动字成,字成指动:任你如何至诚,如何机智,难叫他收回成命消去半行,任你眼泪流完也难洗掉一字。"此句可能是讲旧约《但以理书 5:5》中的情景:巴比伦王伯撒沙设盛宴与一千大臣彻夜狂饮,忽见灯台对面墙上有指头在写字,他大惊失色,叫来先知但以理解释墙上的字。当夜伯撒沙王被杀,巴比伦国灭亡。

(译注/唐毅)

Domestick Greatness Unattainable
近观无伟人

By *Samuel Johnson*
文/塞缪尔·约翰逊　译/唐毅

译者按：塞缪尔·约翰逊（1709—1784），英国著名散文家、诗人、文学评论家以及词典编纂者。主编了《英语大辞典》和《莎士比亚集》，在英国文学史上享有极高的声誉。本文选自他主编的周刊 *Idler* 第 51 期。作为新古典主义的代表人物，塞缪尔·约翰逊在散文中也追求"和谐、匀称、平衡、节制"，此外他用词精炼老道，善用格言警句，常常妙语频出，翻译时应注意保持用词简练，语言老道的风格。

It has been commonly remarked, that eminent men are least eminent at home, that bright characters lose much of their splendor at a nearer view, and many, who fill the world with their fame, excite very little reverence among those that surround them in their domestick privacies.

To blame or suspect is easy and natural. When the fact is evident, and the cause doubtful, some accusation is always engendered between idleness and malignity. This disparity of general and familiar esteem is, therefore,

常有人说，声名显赫者在家最不起眼。于近处观，熠熠生辉的名人光环不再。世上许多声名显赫之人，私下生活中却很少让身边人敬畏。

责备或怀疑一个人很容易，也合乎常理。当事实明确，原因却不甚了了时，就会有人或因无聊，或出于恶意而加以指责。因此，人们认为，这种公众名望和熟人圈内的名声好坏之别，是因为其人有过

imputed to hidden vices, and to practices indulged in secret, but carefully covered from the publick eye[1].

  Vice will indeed always produce contempt. The dignity of Alexander[2], though nations fell prostrated before him, was certainly held in little veneration by the partakers of his midnight revels, who had seen him, in the madness of wine, murder his friend, or set fire to the Persian palace at the instigation of a harlot[3]; and it is well remembered among us, that the avarice of Marlborough[4] kept him in subjection to his wife, while he was dreaded by France as her conqueror, and honoured by the emperor as his deliverer.

  But though, where there is vice there must be want of reverence, it is not reciprocally true, that where there is want of reverence there is always vice. That awe which great actions or abilities impress will be inevitably diminished by acquaintance, though nothing either mean or criminal should be found.

  Of men, as of every thing else, we must judge according to our knowledge[5]. When we see of a hero only his battles, or of a writer only his books, we have nothing to allay our ideas of their greatness. We consider the one only as the guardian of his country, and the other only as the instructor of mankind. We have neither opportunity nor motive to examine

不为人知的恶行，或是暗中沉湎于不良嗜好，只是小心遮掩起来不为公众所知而已。

  恶行确实总会遭人鄙视。虽然各国都向亚历山大大帝俯首称臣，但和他一起深夜狂欢作乐的人，却很少会敬重他。因为他们见过他趁着酒劲谋杀自己的朋友，见过他受妓女唆使放火烧毁波斯宫殿。我们也都清楚记得，马尔伯勒公爵征服了法兰西，让法国人闻风丧胆，又被国王敬为救星，而他却因贪婪对妻子言听计从。

  作恶必然导致威望尽失，但是反之不然，即丧失威望不一定因为作恶。一个因雄功伟业或旷世之才而令世人钦佩的人，即使未曾有过卑劣之举或犯罪行径，人们对他的敬畏也会因了解而减少。

  和评判其他事物一样，对人的评价亦需凭借我们对其人的了解。一位英雄，如果我们只看他的战功，一位作家，如果我们只看他的作品，便不会有什么来破坏他们在我们心目中的伟大形象。我们会视英雄为国家的守护者，视作家为人类的导师。我们没有机会，亦不想去考察他们生活中更加微不足道的那一

Domestick Greatness Unattainable

the minuter parts of their lives, or the less apparent peculiarities of their characters; we name them with habitual respect, and forget, what we still continue to know, that they are men like other mortals.

But such is the constitution of the world, that much of life must be spent in the same manner by the wise and the ignorant, the exalted and the low. Men, however distinguished by external accidents or intrinsic qualities, have all the same wants, the same pains, and, as far as the senses are consulted, the same pleasures. The petty cares and petty duties are the same in every station to every understanding[6], and every hour brings some occasion on which we all sink to the common level. We are all naked till we are dressed, and hungry till we are fed; and the general's triumph, and sage's disputation, end, like the humble labours of the smith or ploughman, in a dinner or in sleep.

Those notions which are to be collected by reason, in opposition to the senses, will seldom stand forward in the mind, but lie treasured in the remoter repositories of memory, to be found only when they are sought. Whatever any man may have written or done, his precepts or his valour will scarcely overbalance the unimportant uniformity which runs through his time. We do not easily consider him as great, whom our own eyes show us to be little; nor labour to keep

部分，更不会去考察他们性格中不那么显著的品质。每当提到他们的名字，我们会习以为常地心怀敬意，却忘了他们和其他人一样也是凡人——其实我们现在仍需明白这一点。

世事即是如此。无论鸿儒还是白丁、显贵还是走卒，大多数时候人都过着相同的生活。一个人，无论成就多大，品德多么高尚，但只要他们是用感官来感知，他们其实都有同样的需求、同样的痛苦和同样的欢愉。无论何人，身居何位，都一样要处理琐碎的事务、承担琐碎的责任，每一时刻都会发生一些状况让我们陷入相同的境地。正如穿衣之前，我们都浑身赤裸；吃饭之前，我们都饥肠辘辘；将军凯旋，圣贤论争，其实与铁匠或农夫的卑贱劳动并无二致，最后都会以吃饭睡觉而终。

那些理性的想法不同于感官认识，很少显之于心，而是埋藏于记忆宝库的深处，唯有追想之时，才能寻获。无论别人如何以文鼓动，以身示范，世人达成何种默契，而他的想法和勇气都很少会折服于此，因为于他而言实属无关紧要。我们不太会视他为伟人，因为在我们眼里他是渺小的；我们也不会努力去发现他那些潜藏的优秀品质，因为他和我们一样有不少弱点，干了不少蠢事。和我

present to our thoughts the latent excellencies of him, who shares with us all our weaknesses and many of our follies; who, like us, is delighted with slight amusements, busied with trifling employments, and disturbed by little vexations[7].

Great powers cannot be exerted, but when great exigencies make them necessary. Great exigencies can happen but seldom, and therefore, those qualities which have a claim to the veneration of mankind, lie hid, for the most part, like subterranean treasures, over which the foot passes as on common ground, till necessity breaks open the golden cavern.

In the ancient celebration of victory, a slave was placed on the triumphal car, by the side of the general, who reminded him by a short sentence, that he was a man. Whatever danger there might be lest a leader, in his passage to the capitol[8], should forget the frailties of his nature, there was surely no need of such an admonition; the intoxication could not have continued long; he would have been at home but a few hours, before some of his dependants would have forgot his greatness, and shown him, that, notwithstanding his laurels, he was yet a man.

There are some who try to escape this domestick degradation, by laboring to appear always wise or always great; but he that strives against nature, will for ever strive in vain. To be grave of mien and slow of utterance; to look

们一样,他也为一点小事而乐,为琐碎的工作奔忙,也被小小烦恼所困扰。

唯有危急之时,雄才大略才有用武之地。危急时刻不常有,因此那些让人敬仰的品质大都深藏不露。大多数的情况下,它们如同深埋于地下的宝藏,我们从上面经过,只当踩着普通的地面,直到情势所迫,黄金洞窟才被人打开。

古代人们庆祝胜利之时,会将一个奴隶放在凯旋而归的战车上,立于将军身旁,还会用简短的话提醒将军他依然是个凡人。在前往朱庇特神庙途中,唯恐将军忘记本性中的弱点而出现危险,其实也大可不必如此谏言。他的自我陶醉不会持续太久,数小时后便要回到家中。家人早已忘掉他的所有伟大,只会让他明白,尽管荣誉有加,他不过还是一介凡夫。

有些人不愿在家纡尊降贵,尽力显出一贯智慧、永远伟大的样子来。但此举有违本性,亦是徒劳。表面上神态严肃,讷于言语;目光关切,言谈谨慎,这些均可刻意而为。但无需质疑之时炫耀智

with solicitude and speak with hesitation, is attainable at will; but the show of wisdom is ridiculous when there is nothing to cause doubt, as that of valour where there is nothing to be feared.

　　A man who has duly considered the condition of his being, will contentedly yield to the course of things; he will not pant for distinction where distinction would imply no merit; but though on great occasions he may wish to be greater than others, he will be satisfied in common occurrences not to be less.

慧，无可畏惧之际，炫耀勇气，则贻笑大方也。

　　有自知之明者安于天命，顺其自然。他明白名气并非德行，因而不会孜孜以求。虽然在重大场合，他亦有出人头地之愿望，而在平常，他亦可甘于默默无闻。

注释：

1. 此句的主要结构是被动结构。为了符合汉语的表达习惯，译者将原文的被动结构转换为主动结构进行表达，增补了被动结构的主语"人们"。此外，be imputed to 表示"把……归因于……"的意思，通过增补的主语将其译为"人们认为，……是因为……"。如此一来，将被动语句转换为主动语句，译文就更加自然、流畅。另外，general 和 familiar 分别表达"在公众中"和"在熟悉的人中"，翻译时需要将意思增补出来，不能直接翻译为"普遍的名望和熟悉的名望"，否则，译文的意思令人费解。

2. 指亚历山大大帝（公元前 356—前 323），即亚历山大三世，马其顿王国（亚历山大帝国）国王，世界古代史上著名的军事家和政治家，是欧洲历史上最伟大的四大军事统帅之首（亚历山大大帝、汉尼拔·巴卡、恺撒大帝、拿破仑）。

3. 从语法上来说，此非限制性定语从句虽然是修饰说明 the partakers，但从意义上来说，也是说明这些 partakers 不敬重亚历山大大帝的原因，所以译文增补了"因为"一词，来说明原因。

4. 第一代马尔伯勒公爵（1650—1722），名约翰·丘吉尔，英国军事家、政治家，在西班牙王位继承战争中大展神威，成为近代欧洲最出色的将领之一。

5. knowledge 在此是表示"了解"之意，不能翻译为"知识"。

6. 这里的 station 指"地位",understanding 指代"人",故而翻译为"无论何人,身居何位"。

7. 此句比较长,包含有三个定语从句。从语法上来看,定语从句修饰的主句提到了 him(他),但是从语义上看,定语从句也是说明为何我们不会将 him(他)视为伟人。译者据此增加了"因为"一词,使表达的意思更加明确,层次更加清楚。

8. 指朱庇特神庙。

(译注/唐毅)

Kunqu Opera, The Peony Pavilion
昆曲《牡丹亭》

By Anne Ozorio
文/安妮·奥佐里奥　译/唐毅

译者按: 此文主要面向西方读者介绍中国著名的昆曲《牡丹亭》,而昆曲——这一中国传统的戏曲形式,西方读者无疑是陌生的,即使是现代的中国人大多也未必了解。因此,作者以《牡丹亭》为例,对昆曲的诞生、表现手法、舞台表现等都一一做了介绍。为了说明昆曲这种较为小众的艺术形式,让西方读者更容易理解,作者用西方读者熟悉的《罗密欧与朱丽叶》、芭蕾舞等来进行比较说明。本文以说明为主,因涉及的话题具有一定的专业性,翻译时要注意准确地翻译相关的艺术概念和专业术语,否则会影响译文的准确性。

Kunqu Opera emerged as a distinct form six hundred years ago, at the beginning of the Ming Dynasty but it builds on centuries of art long before that. For many, Kunqu epitomises the ultimate in artistic refinement because it unites so many sophisticated genres, such as literature, history, music, dance, ethics. To understand Chinese aesthetics, study Kunqu.

The Peony Pavilion, or *Mudan Ting* in Chinese, is a story every Chinese knows, It's

昆曲,作为一种独特的形式,诞生于600年前的明初,而它所传承的艺术传统早已形成,积淀了几个世纪。对许多人来说,昆曲代表的是艺术精雕的极致,它集文学、历史、音乐、舞蹈和伦理等众多复杂门类于一体。要理解中国美学,就要研究昆曲。

《牡丹亭》的故事在中国人人皆知。它是伟大的学者汤显祖1598年创作的一

based on a novel written in 1598 by the great scholar Tang Xianzu, a huge sprawling work in the style of classic Ming literature, full of references to poetry, history and philosophy. The original opera lasts over 20 hours, with over 100 arias and other set pieces. In the past, most educated people would have known the background well enough that they could pick up on the many connotations and allusions, gaining extended pleasure beyond what they saw and heard on stage. Nonetheless, Chinese opera[1] is by no means elitist. Until fairly recently, most rural Chinese were illiterate, yet opera in some form was standard entertainment. There's nothing to stop people having a good time with Chinese opera even if they know nothing of Chinese culture.

  Kunqu is surprisingly[2] modern because it addresses universal human feelings. Tang Xianzu, the author of *The Peony Pavilion*, understood the significance of dreams and inner emotion long before Freud wrote his psychology. Tang wrote what are now called "The Four Dreams", namely, *Legend of the Purple Hair Pin*, *The Peony Pavilion*, *Dream of Nanke*, and *Dream of Handan*, four novels which involve dreams and are an essential part of the Kunqu canon.

  Kunqu opera also illustrates other principles of Chinese art. In Chinese painting, for example, blank spaces[3] are an essential part of

部戏剧。这部鸿篇巨著具有明代文学的古典风格,引用了许多诗歌、历史和哲学的内容。最初整部戏长达20多个小时,有100多个唱段和其他固定曲子。过去,大多数受过教育的人非常了解这部戏的背景,因此他们能够听懂曲子的内涵和所用的典故,从而获得比更多的愉悦,远超舞台所观所闻。然而,中国戏曲绝不是社会精英的专属。直到近代,大部分生活在中国农村的人还目不识丁,然而某种形式的戏曲却是他们最正常不过的娱乐方式。即使对中国文化一无所知,也不妨碍人们好好欣赏中国戏曲。

  昆曲的现代性令人惊异,因为它往往关注的是人类共有的情感。早在弗洛伊德写出他的心理学著作之前,《牡丹亭》的作者汤显祖就懂得了梦境和内心情感的意义。汤氏写过如今名为"临川四梦"系列的书,即《紫钗记》《牡丹亭》《南柯记》和《邯郸记》。这四部戏剧均涉及有关梦境的内容,构成了昆曲的核心。

  昆曲也阐释了中国艺术的其他原则。例如,留白是国画创作的一个重要部分。同理,中式园林被设计成迷你版

Kunqu Opera, The Peony Pavilion

the composition. Similarly, Chinese gardens are designed to represent miniature vistas from landscape. A kunqu stage isn't cluttered with scenery[4]. A group of soldiers stand in formation, some with oars, which they move in swift unison, while the orchestra builds up fast rhythmic crescendi. The combination of music and movement creates an image of huge armies descending down river. The sedan chair in which the elderly gardener is carried is "formed" instantly when the Imperial Guards lower their banners to make two planks. The gardener sits on one, his feet resting on the other. His expression and joyful singing show how thrilled he is at being so honoured. You don't need to see the details[5], you can hear them.

The spirits of nature and of the garden are conveyed by actors dressed in silk, ornately embroidered with flowers. They fill the stage, their sleeves[6] fluttering and swaying. Flowers move in the breeze, and fragrance is invisible. How beautifully these dancers convey the sensual lushness of a real garden! No painted backdrop can compare. Even the splendour of the Emperor's chamber is suggested not by artefacts but by the costumes and demeanour of his entourage. This timeless, elegant simplicity is effective because it concentrates attention on the singing[7] and music. There are parallels with Greek tragedy and early European theatre. The

的自然景观。昆曲的舞台不会到处布景。士兵列队而立,一些士兵手握船桨,敏捷地划桨,动作整齐划一,而乐队奏出节奏明快、逐渐增强的音乐。乐曲和动作共同营造出大军顺流而下的意象。放低旗帜,禁卫军即可变旗为板,变出供年迈园丁乘坐的轿子。园丁坐在其中的一块板子上,双脚放在另外一块上面。他脸部的表情和欢快地唱曲表明,他因礼遇有加而欣喜万分。因此,无须眼观,耳听即可了解剧情。

自然和花园的神韵是由穿着绣有花朵刺绣丝绸戏服的演员传递的。台上,水袖飘舞,微风习习,花儿摇曳,暗香浮动。这些舞者将花园的活色生香、花团锦簇表达得多么传神啊! 这是画制的背景完全无法媲美的。即使是皇帝寝宫的金碧辉煌也并非由人工装饰营造而成,而是由皇帝随从的戏服以及举止来体现的。这种简朴的表达、优雅不受制于时间,而聚焦于唱腔和乐曲。这与希腊的悲剧和欧洲早期的戏剧有许多相似之处。从某种程度上说,戏曲"必须"写实的实说法其实近来才

assumption that opera "has" somehow to be literal[8] is very recent indeed and by no means the norm. Kunqu shows just how effective minimalism can be. Significantly, Chinese opera was fashionable in the west in the 1920's and 30's when European theatre was undergoing a transformation. Bertholt Brecht, for example, was said to admire Mei Lanfang, perhaps the most famous Chinese opera star in modern times.

Expression in Kunqu opera always derives from the human form, not from mechanical devices like scenery. There are hundreds of different gestures, creating a whole extra language for communication. Finger movements are exquisitely subtle. It makes a difference how they are arranged and how they move. Similarly, when an actor holds his foot in a certain angle, it can indicate setting out on a long journey, or an arduous climb. Audiences learn to "read" these clues quite easily, just as ballet audiences quickly pick up on the stylised gestures in dance.

Every gesture serves a purpose. Movement is extremely fluid and graceful, so when the actors do stop and hold a pose, it's significant. One unique feature of Chinese opera is shuixiu, or "water sleeves", where the very clothes people wear become an extension of meaning. For example, quietly flipping the sleeve ends over indicates alertness. Letting the sleeves

出现，绝非常态。昆曲说明，极简主义可以极富感染力。有意思的是，中国戏曲在1920年代和30年代的西方非常盛行，那时西方的戏剧正在经历变革。据说，当时的贝尔托特·布雷赫特夫人就对现代中国最负有盛名的戏剧明星梅兰芳仰慕不已。

昆曲中的表演总是通过人体形态而非舞台布景这样的机械装置来体现。昆曲中成百上千的不同手势，形成了一整套非语言的交流体系。手指的运动非常微妙讲究。不同手势和动作可以表达不同的含义。同样，当演员的脚以一定的角度站立时，就表示其即将远行，或将奋力攀登。观众很容易就学会"读懂"这些暗示，就像芭蕾舞观众很快就领会舞蹈中的一些典型姿势一样。

每一个手势都有其用处。演员动作行云流水，优美雅致，因此当他们停下，保持一个姿势不动的时候，就值得注意。水袖是中国戏曲独有的，正是演员身着的这块布将剧情的含义延伸。比如，轻轻翻转袖口，表示警觉；让袖子水平地抖动，就营造出一种空间上的持续移动。手势包含一整套语汇，但是技巧在于演

Kunqu Opera, The Peony Pavilion

flutter horizontally creates the impression of sustained movement over space. There's a whole vocabulary of gesture, but the skill comes from how an individual actor uses them in combination. The scene in which the young scholar ventures out into the world and is tossed by a storm was remarkably vivid because Yu Jiulin, who played the role, managed to "act with his sleeves", so they seemed at once part of him and yet part of the wind and the rain beating on him. It was a tour de force, though only one of many in this fine production. This demonstrates one of the reasons why Chinese opera endures so well. Within the stylisation, there's room for spontaneity and personal freedom.

Chinese music isn't fixed into notation like Western music. Again, it uses a language of gestures like the actors do, varying and adapting to the action on stage. It's closer to improvisation, because the aim is perfect coordination between action and sound. When the percussion beats a steady sequence gradually increasing in speed, it can indicate something is about to happen before it does. Chinese opera orchestras are like giant chamber ensembles, interacting with the singers and actors as well as with each other. There were fewer than twenty musicians in the pit yet their range was huge. Sometimes all you would hear was a single, plaintive ocarina, as silent and as poignant as a

员个体如何综合运用各种手势。有一场戏是年轻书生离家闯荡，暴雨阻路，演员俞玖林的精彩表演让这场戏格外生动，他娴熟地"运用水袖"，使其既像身体的一部分，又像刮起的大风和打在身上的雨点。这真是绝技，虽然这仅仅是这部制作精良的戏曲中众多的绝技之一。这也是中国戏曲历久不衰的原因之一：在效仿规定动作的同时，亦有自发的、个性化的自由表演空间。

中国音乐并非如西方音乐那样被固定成符号。与演员运用一系列各式各样的手势语言表演一样，音乐要配合舞台表演而进行变奏。它更接近即兴演奏，因为配乐的目的是要使表演和乐声完美协调。当一连串固定不变的打击乐节奏越来越快时，就预示有事即将发生。中国戏曲的乐队，就像大型的室内乐团，各种乐器间要相互配合，亦要和歌者、演员互相配合。乐池里不到20人，奏出的音乐却很丰富。有时只能听到单一、哀怨的陶笛声，就像一只远处的鸟儿，寂寥而伤感。有时，乐队营造出战场厮杀的混乱骚动，喇叭吹得尖厉刺耳，打击乐奏出马蹄隆隆。中国的

distant bird. At other times, the orchestra could create the tumult of a battle scene, trumpets blaring, percussion evoking thundering hooves. Chinese music proves that atonal and dissonant music is perfectly natural, and capable of expressing profound emotion. Western musicians can learn a lot from these very different approaches to rhythm, tempi and interval.

You don't have to be a scholar or an artist to appreciate Kunqu. Kunqu opera is universal because it appeals on a direct human, emotional level, accessible to anyone who opens their heart.

音乐证明,无调和不和谐的乐音完全可以处理得很自然,可以表达出深邃的情感。对西方音乐家来说,这些对节奏、拍子和音程迥然不同的处理方法有很多值得借鉴的地方。

欣赏昆曲,并不要求观众学识渊博或擅长艺术。昆曲直接唤起人的情感,只要你敞开心扉,就可以欣赏昆曲,因此昆曲是一种具有普世价值的艺术。

注释:

1. 歌剧是西方的舞台表演艺术,是完全用歌唱和音乐来表现剧情的戏剧。在古代,中国没有歌剧这一艺术形式,因此,Chinese Opera 不能翻译为"中国歌剧",而应翻译为"中国戏曲"。

2. "surprisingly"一词修饰后面的形容词,如果不将其分拆出来,译文读起来就会比较拗口,不流畅。

3. blank spaces 的字面意思是指"空白的空间"。但用于中国画创作时,指的是"留白"。中国画注重营造意境,常常通过留白来烘托意境。

4. scenery 原意是指"风景",但在此处表示舞台上的布景。

5. detail 在字典中的解释是"细节"。但根据上下文,此处应该指正在演出的"剧情"。由此可见,词的含义与语境关系密切,不依据语境来确定词义,容易产生语义不清的后果,翻译时尤其要注意这一点。

6. sleeves 是一个普通名词,表示衣袖。在中国戏曲表演中,通常叫作"水袖"。在中国戏曲的舞台上,水袖是极具表达功能的一种方式。甩水袖的不同方式,可以表达不同的含义。

7. 同理,中国戏曲舞台的歌唱,应该译为"唱腔"。

8. literal 一词有多种含义,比如"逐字的""字面意思的""只讲究实际的""如实的、不夸张的"等等,译者翻译时比较难以确定词义。通过查阅有关昆曲艺术的资料,可以了解到昆曲的舞台布景非常简单,主要利用演员的唱腔、身段、手势等进行写意式的表达。据此,可以判断,此处的 literal 应该是"如实的"之意,故译为"写实的"。

(译注/唐毅)

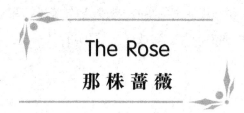

The Rose
那株蔷薇

By *Logan Pearsall Smith*

文/洛根·皮尔索尔·史密斯　译/唐毅

译者按：洛根·皮尔索尔·史密斯（1865—1946）系英国散文家和评论家。此文选自作者1918年出版的《小品集》(*The Trivia*)。文学作品的翻译往往与作品的主题密切相关，对主题的解读会影响到译文中的基本要素，如背景、象征等的翻译。本文中对Rose一词的翻译即是如此。Rose在此文中就是爱情的象征，它不仅是伯爵追求爱情的象征，也是作者表达对爱情的看法的一个象征。据此译者将Rose翻译为蔷薇，而不是玫瑰，主要因为以下原因：第一，在英文中rose既可以指玫瑰，又可以指蔷薇。但是玫瑰不是攀缘植物，而蔷薇是。另外，根据英汉大词典的解释，rose tree 是指独干蔷薇。第二，虽然玫瑰和蔷薇属于同一科目，在英语中也是用同一个词来表示，但在汉语中是由不同的词来表达的，所以文中的rose到底为玫瑰还是蔷薇，对汉语读者来说还是有困扰的。正如文章主题所诠释的，伯爵和意大利小姐的爱并非真爱。虽然伯爵非常爱她，后来种植蔷薇也是为了纪念这段感情。但显然那位小姐并不爱伯爵。可见，伯爵为爱孤独一生，以为自己追求的是真爱（玫瑰），其实不然。他所追求的不是真爱，而是爱的幻觉（蔷薇）。正如蔷薇不是玫瑰，但是很像玫瑰。作者想要通过这个故事表达这样的观点：真爱——犹如黎明时分的山上小城，像闪烁的繁星一样美而缥缈，可望而不可得也。由此可见，对此文中主要的象征rose一词的翻译，离不开对文章主题的领会和解读。此外作者用简单的语言将这样一个失败的爱情故事娓娓道来，看似轻松自然，其实意蕴深厚、意味悠长。翻译时应注意保持文章简单朴素、但又令人回味无穷的风格。

The Rose

The old lady had always been proud of the great rose-tree in her garden, and was fond of telling how it had grown from a cutting she had brought years before from Italy, when she was first married[1]. She and her husband had been travelling back in their carriage from Rome (it was before the time of railways), and on a bad piece of road south of Siena they had broken down, and had been forced to pass the night in a little house by the roadside. The accommodation was wretched of course; she had spent a sleepless night, and rising early and stood, wrapped up, at her window, with the cool air blowing on her face, to watch the dawn. She could still, after all these years, remember the blue mountains with the bright moon above them, and how a far-off town on one of the peaks had gradually grown whiter and whiter, till the moon faded, the mountains were touched with the pink of the rising sun, and suddenly the town was lit as by illumination, one window after another catching and reflecting the sun's beams, till at last the whole little city twinkled and sparkled up in the sky like a nest of stars.

That morning, finding they would have to wait while their carriage was being repaired, they had driven in a local conveyance up to the city on the mountain, where they had been told they would find better quarters; and there they had stayed two or three days. It was one of the

老妇人素以花园里那颗大大的蔷薇树为荣,总是津津乐道地告诉别人蔷薇树是多年前她从意大利带回的枝条插枝长成的。那是她初婚的时候,和丈夫坐着马车从罗马旅行归来(当时还没有铁路)。在锡耶纳南面一条糟糕的路上,车坏了,他们只好在路边的一间小房子里过夜。自然,小房子里住宿条件很差。她一夜无眠,早早穿衣起床,站在窗边观看黎明的景色。凉风习习,吹拂着她的脸。多年之后,她依然记得,一轮明月悬在黛色的群山之上。她看着远远矗立在一座山峰上的小镇,一点一点地泛白,直到月亮渐渐消失,周围的群山被冉冉升起的太阳染上一抹粉色。刹那间,小镇好像被光突然点亮似的,一扇窗,又一扇窗,在阳光的照射下,反射着太阳的光辉。直到最后,整个小城像一群繁星,在天上一闪一闪地闪亮。

那天清晨,马车送去修理,想到不得不在此停留,于是他们驾了一辆当地的车子向山上的小城驶去。据说在小城里可以找到更好的住处。于是他们在那里停留了两三天。这是一座典型的意大利小城,高耸的教堂,装饰浮华的广场,窄窄的

miniature Italian cities with a high church, a pretentious piazza, a few narrow streets and little palaces, perched, all compact and complete, on the top of a mountain, within an enclosure of walls hardly larger than an English kitchen garden. But it was full of life and noise, echoing all day and all night with the sounds of feet and voices.

The café of the simple inn where they stayed was the meeting-place of the notabilities of the little city; the *Sindaco*, the avvocato, the doctor, and a few others; and among them they noticed a beautiful, slim, talkative old man, with bright black eyes and snowwhite hair[2]—tall and straight and still with the figure of a youth, although the waiter told them with pride that the *Conte* was *molto vechio*—would in fact be eighty in the following year. He was the last of his family, the waiter added—they had once been great and rich people—but he had no descendants; in fact the waiter mentioned with complacency, as if it were a story on which the locality prided itself, that the *Conte* had been unfortunate in love, and had never married.

The old gentleman, however, seemed cheerful enough; and it was plain that he took an interest in the strangers, and wished to make their acquaintance. This was soon effected by the friendly waiter; and after a little talk the old man invited them to visit his villa and garden which were just outside the walls of the town.

几条街道和几个小小的宫殿,全都紧凑地栖在山顶上的四面围墙里。虽然围墙内的面积几乎只有英国人厨房后的菜地一样大,但却是人声鼎沸,脚步声和说话声昼夜回响。

他们住的旅店里有个小餐厅是小城名流聚会的地方,有市长、法官、医生,还有一些别的人;在这些人中间,一位很健谈的老人引起了他们的注意。老人长得英俊、瘦削,双目乌黑明亮,白发似雪。侍者颇有些骄傲地告诉他们,伯爵年纪很大了。确实下一年他就80岁了,但老人高高挺拔的身材,和年轻人一样。侍者接着说道,伯爵家族就剩他一个人了。他们家原来是望族,非常富有,可是他没有后代,因为伯爵在爱情方面很是不幸,他一直单身。尽管如此,侍者讲的时候,语气甚是得意,好像当地人对此都感到自豪。

可是,这位老绅士看起来很开心,而且显然他对陌生来客感兴趣,想和他们认识一下。很快,善解人意的侍者为他们牵线搭桥。聊了一会,老人就邀请他们去做客,参观他在城墙外的别墅和花园。因此,第二天下午,当太阳开始西下,从旅店的门廊和窗户望出去,蓝色的阴影开始撒

The Rose

So the next afternoon, when the sun began to descend, and they saw in glimpses through doorways and windows, blue shadows beginning to spread over the brown mountains, they went to pay their visit. It was not much of a place, a small, modernish, stucco villa, with a hot pebbly garden, and in it a stone basin with torpid gold fish, and a statue of Diana[3] and her hounds against the wall. But what gave a glory to it was a gigantic rose-tree which clambered over the house, almost smothering the windows, and filling the air with the perfume of its sweetness. Yes, it was a fine rose, the *Conte* said proudly when they praised it, and he would tell the *Signora* about it. And as they sat there, drinking the wine he offered them, he alluded with the cheerful indifference of old age to his love affair, as though he took for granted that they had heard of it already.

"The lady lived across the valley there beyond that hill. I was a young man then, for it was many years ago. I used to ride over to see her; it was a long way, but I rode fast, for young men, as no doubt the *Signora* knows, are impatient. But the lady was not kind[4], she would keep me waiting, oh, for hours; and one day when I had waited very long I grew very angry, and as I walked up and down in the garden where she had told me she would see me, I broke one of her roses, broke a branch from it; and when I saw what I had done, I hid

布在褐色的群山上时,他们就出门去拜访老人。这个小小的乡村别墅谈不上奢华,石灰泥的外墙,有些现代感。别墅带有一个鹅卵石铺就的小花园,花园里有点热。花园里,有一个石头砌成的大盆,金鱼在里面慵懒地游来游去,靠墙处还有一个雕塑,是狩猎女神狄安娜和她的猎犬。然而,让别墅夺目生辉的是一颗巨大的蔷薇树,蔷薇攀缘在别墅之上,几乎将窗户全都遮住了,空气中弥漫着蔷薇花甜甜的香气。听到他们赞美这株蔷薇,伯爵得意地说道,不错,这株蔷薇确实长得很漂亮,他很乐意给夫人讲讲这株蔷薇的故事。于是,他们在花园坐下,喝着伯爵拿来的葡萄酒。伯爵由衷地用老年人才有的淡然神情将年轻时的情事娓娓道来,似乎以为他们对此早有耳闻。

"那位小姐住在山那边的峡谷对面。那是多年以前了,我还很年轻。我常常骑马翻山去看她;路途很远,但我骑得很快。夫人,你一定明白,年轻小伙子都是性急的。可是那位小姐不太体贴,总是让我等啊等,等上几个小时。有一天,我已经等了很长时间,等得很生气。因为她说会在她家的花园里见我,于是我就在花园里走来走去,折断一株蔷薇,又将这支蔷薇上的一根树枝折断,然后将枝条藏在外套里面。就这样,回到家,将它种下。夫人,你

it inside my coat—so—; and when I came home I planted it, and the *Signora* sees how it has grown. If the *Signora* admires it, I must give her a cutting to plant also in her garden; I am told the English have beautiful gardens that are green, and not burnt with the sun like ours."

The next day, when their mended carriage had come up to fetch them, and they were just starting to drive away from the inn, the *Conte's* old servant appeared with the rose-cutting neatly wrapped up, and the compliments and wishes for a *buon viaggio* from her master. The town collected to see them depart, and the children ran after their carriage through the gate of the little city. They heard a rush of feet behind them for a few moments, but soon they were far down toward the valley; the little town with all its noise and life was high above them on its mountain peak.

She had planted the rose at home, where it had grown and flourished in a wonderful manner; and every June the great mass of leaves and shoots still broke out into a passionate splendor of scent and crimson colour, as if in its root and fibres[5] there still burnt the anger and thwarted desire of that Italian lover. Of course, the old *Conte* must have died many years ago; she had forgotten his name, and had even forgotten the name of the mountain city that she had stayed in, after first

看它已长大成树。要是夫人喜欢,我就剪下一支送给她,让她也种在花园里。别人告诉过我,英国人的花园总是一片翠绿,漂亮极了,可不像我们的花园,被太阳烤焦了似的。"

第二天,修好的马车上山来接他们。正要从小旅店驾车启程时,伯爵的老仆来了,手里拿着一枝包裹得整整齐齐的蔷薇。她转达了主人的问候,并祝他们一路顺风。全城的人都来为他们送行。孩子们追着他们的马车跑,一直追到小城门外,车驶了好一阵都还能听到身后急切的跑步声。但很快他们就下山往山谷去了。小城的喧闹和生活都留在了高高的山顶之上。

她将那株蔷薇种在家里,蔷薇茁壮成长,花朵绚烂,每到六月,绿叶和嫩芽蓬勃而出,枝繁叶茂。蔷薇花朵猩红艳丽,香气袭人。满树蔷薇看起来热情似火,仿佛树根中、根根枝条上,仍然燃烧着那位意大利情人的熊熊怒火和受挫的爱意。不用说,老伯爵多年前就已过世,她也早已忘了他的名字,甚至也不记得当年住过的小城的名字,唯记得初见时的山上小城,远远地在晨曦中闪烁,灿若繁星。

seeing it twinkling at dawn in the sky, like a nest of stars.

▶ 注释：

1. "first married"通常翻译为"刚刚结婚"。但据译者对本文主题的理解，作者通过文中的两个人物：伯爵和老妇的爱情来凸显爱而不得的主题。"first"也有"第一次"之意，故笔者译为"初婚"，以此暗示老妇人不止一次走进婚姻追求真爱，似乎和老伯爵一样，也是求而不得，从而达到契合主题的目的。

2. 此句较长，形容词较多，如果不加处理，译文容易显得呆板，因此译者将"talkative"首先分拆出来，单独译出，其他几个描述老人外貌的形容词放在一起翻译，这样译文的语义联系更加紧密，表达更清晰。

3. 希腊神话中的狩猎女神。因中国读者可能对此不熟悉，故译者采用增译的方法，将狄安娜是谁直接说明，方便读者阅读。

4. kind 一词做形容词时有多种含义。如果选择"善良"的词义，不太符合文章本意。毕竟年轻伯爵当时不会觉得所爱之人不善良，而是不够体贴。据英汉大词典的释义，kind 可表示"considerate"之意，意为"think about other people's feelings, and careful not to do anything that will upset them"，此词条的含义更符合原文的意思。由此可见，翻译时即使是很常见的普通词，也需要认真对待，不能掉以轻心。

5. 此处的 fibers 指的是植物的须根或细枝。

（译注/唐毅）

How We Kept Mother's Day
我们怎样庆祝母亲节

By *Stephen Leacock*
文/ 斯蒂芬·利科克　译/唐毅

译者按：斯蒂芬·利科克（1869—1944），加拿大作家。他涉猎广泛、作品众多。所写文章涵盖社会、政治、经济、科学、历史、幽默小说和文学评论等。在20世纪早期，被视为英语国家最幽默的作家并广受欢迎。作者以第一人称的视角讲述了"我们"一家人本来想利用母亲节让母亲在这一天从家务中解脱出来，享受节日，结果却是家中每个人都驾车出游，非常开心地度过了一天，只留下母亲在家继续为他们烧饭忙碌。作者的描写幽默中透出温情，轻松中带有讽刺，读来别有趣味，让人啼笑皆非。此外，本文语言简单朴实，较为口语化。翻译时，要注意传达这种风格。

Of all the different ideas that have been started lately, I think that the very best is the notion of celebrating once a year "Mother's Day". I don't wonder that May the eleventh is becoming such a popular date all over America and I am sure the idea will spread to England too.

It is specially in a big family like ours that such an idea takes hold[1]. So we decided to have a special celebration of Mother's Day. We thought it a fine idea. It made us all realize how

在最近提出来的各种倡议中，我觉得最好的是庆祝一年一度的"母亲节"。我并不奇怪5月11号这一天在整个美国成为如此受欢迎的一天，我确信这个倡议也会传到英国。

尤其在我们这样的大家庭，这样的倡议很受欢迎。我们决定要以一个特别的方式庆祝母亲节。大家都觉得这个想法不错。庆祝母亲节能使我们大

How We Kept Mother's Day

much Mother had done for us for years and all the efforts[2] and sacrifice that she had made for our sake.

So we decided that we'd make it a great day, a holiday for all the family, and do everything we could to make Mother happy. Father decided to take a holiday from his office, so as to help in celebrating the day, and my sister Anne and I stayed at home from college classes, and Mary and my brother Will stayed at home from High School.

It was our plan to make it a day just like Christmas or any big holidays, and so we decided to decorate the house with flowers and with mottoes over the mantelpieces[3], and all that kind of things. We got Mother to make mottoes and arrange the decoration, because she always does it at Christmas.

The two girls thought it would be a nice thing to dress in our very best for such a big occasion, and so they both got new hats. Mother trimmed both the hats, and they looked fine, and Father had bought four-in-hand silk ties[4] for himself and us boys as a souvenir of the day to remember Mother by[5]. We were going to get Mother a new hat too[6], but it turned out that she seemed to really like her old grey bonnet better than a new one, and both the girls said that it was awfully becoming to her.

Well, after breakfast we had it arranged as a surprise for Mother that we would hire a

家意识到母亲年复一年地为我们做了多少，为我们耗费的所有精力和做出的牺牲。

于是我们决定要隆重地度过这一天，把它过成全家人的节日，尽我们所能让母亲快乐。为了帮忙准备庆祝母亲节，父亲决定请一天假，我和姐姐安娜都不去大学上课，读高中的玛丽和弟弟威尔也不去上学了，大家都待在家里。

我们计划要把母亲节搞得像圣诞节之类的大节日一样隆重，所以决定要装饰一下屋子，摆上鲜花，壁炉上方要有格言警句，还有其他的各种装饰。格言警句、屋里的装饰，我们都让妈妈去准备，因为每逢圣诞节这些事都是她做的。

姑娘们觉得这么隆重的节日，得打扮得漂漂亮亮的才行，所以她们俩都买了新的帽子。妈妈又将两顶帽子装点了一下，看起来很漂亮。爸爸早就为我们两个男孩和他自己买好了丝质领带，以此作为节日纪念品来记住妈妈对他们的照顾和情意。我们也打算给妈妈买一顶新帽子，但好像妈妈真的更喜欢她那顶灰色的旧帽子，而且姑娘们也说妈妈戴那顶旧帽子真的很漂亮。

对了，早餐后我们还为妈妈准备了一个惊喜：我们要租一辆车，载她一路到乡

motor car and take her for a beautiful drive away into the country. Mother is hardly ever able to have a treat like that, because we can only afford to keep one maid, and so Mother is busy in the house nearly all the time. And of course the country is so lovely now that it would be just grand for her to have a lovely morning, driving for miles and miles.

But on the very morning of the day we changed the plan a little bit, because it occurred to Father that a thing it would be better to do even than to take Mother for a motor drive would be to take her fishing. Father said that as the car was hired and paid for, we might just as well use it for a drive up into the hills where the streams are. As Father said[7], if you just go out driving without any objects, you have a sense of aimlessness, but if you are going to fish, there is a definite purpose in front of you to heighten the enjoyment.

So[8] we all felt that it would be nicer for Mother to have a definite purpose; and anyway, it turned out that Father had just got a new rod the day before, which made the idea of fishing all the more appropriate, and he said that Mother could use it if she wanted to; in fact, he said it was practically for her, only[9] Mother said she would much rather watch him fish and not try to fish herself.

So we got everything arranged for the trip, and we got Mother to cut up some sandwiches

下好好兜兜风。妈妈几乎从没有享受过这样的待遇,因为我们家只请得起一个女仆,所以妈妈几乎一直都是在屋里忙来忙去。不用说,这个季节乡下美极了。载着她在美丽的清晨一路兜风,对她来说将会是多大的享受啊!

可是,到了要出发的那天早上,我们的计划有了点小小的变动。爸爸突然想到,带妈妈去兜风还不如带她去钓鱼呢。爸爸说既然车租好了,钱也付了,那就开到山上去玩,山上有溪流。爸爸解释说,如果只是漫无目的地兜风,会感觉很盲目,但要是去钓鱼,就有了一个明确的目标,会更开心。

如此说来,大家也都觉得妈妈应该有一个明确的目标更好;而且,爸爸前一天正好买了一根新钓竿,这样钓鱼更加顺理成章了。爸爸还说如果妈妈想钓鱼,就给她用。他说其实这根鱼竿就是给妈妈买的。只是妈妈说,她倒是宁愿看爸爸钓鱼,自己并不想钓。

就这样出游的一切都安排好了。虽然中午我们肯定还会回家好好吃上一顿,

How We Kept Mother's Day

and make up a sort of lunch in case we got hungry, though of course we were to come back home again to a big dinner in the middle of the day, just like X'mas or New Year's Day. Mother packed it all up in a basket for us ready to go in the motor.

Well, when the car came to the door, it turned out that there hardly seemed as much room in it as we had supposed, because we hadn't reckoned on Father's fishing basket and the rods and the lunch, and it was plain enough that we couldn't all get in.

Father said not to mind him, he said that he could just as well stay home, and that he was sure that he could put in the time working in the garden; he said that there was a lot of rough dirty work that he could do, like digging a trench for the garbage, that would save hiring a man, and so he said that he'd stay home; he said that we were not to let the fact of his not having had a real holiday for three years stand in our way[10]; he wanted us to go right ahead and be happy and have a big day, and not to mind him. He said that he could plug away all day, and in fact he said he'd been a fool to think there'd be any holiday for him.

But of course we all felt that it would never do to let Father stay home, especially as we knew he would make trouble if he did. The two girls, Anne and Mary, would gladly have stayed and helped the maid get dinner, only it

就像圣诞节或是元旦时那样,但我们还是让妈妈切好三明治,再做一点餐食,万一饿了可以吃吃。妈妈将所有的食物都包好放在一个篮子里,待我们准备好了就出发。

车子到了门口,结果没想到它好像不够大,因为事先我们没有算上爸爸的钓鱼篮、钓鱼竿和带上的午餐,显然我们大家不可能全都挤进去。

爸爸说不用管他,他待在家里也行,这样的话他肯定会利用这个时间在花园里干点活;他说,有好多又脏又累的活他可以做做,比如挖条排水沟啦,这样就不用雇人去做了,所以他宁愿待在家里;他还说我们不要觉得三年了他都还没好好度个假而搅了出游的兴致;他希望我们赶紧走,好好乐一乐,不用管他。他说他自己会好好干上一整天活。不过他还说,自己还真有点傻,还想能有个假期。

当然我们都觉得绝对不能让爸爸待在家里,尤其我们都清楚,如果他待在家,不知得弄出多少乱子来。安娜和玛丽两姐妹很乐意帮女仆做做晚饭,只是天气这么好,又买了新帽子,待在家里实在太可

seemed such a pity to, on a lovely day like this, having their new hats[11]. But they both said that Mother had only to say the word, and they'd gladly stay home and work. Will and I would have dropped out, but unfortunately we wouldn't have been any use in getting the dinner.

So in the end it was decided that Mother would stay home and just have a lovely day round the house, and get the dinner. It turned out anyway that Mother doesn't care for fishing, and also it was just a little bit cold and fresh out of doors, though it was lovely and sunny, and Father was rather afraid that Mother might take cold if she came.

He said he would never forgive himself if he dragged Mother round the country and let her take a severe cold at a time when she might be having a beautiful rest. He said it was our duty to try and let Mother get all the rest and quiet that she could, after all that she had done for all of us, and he said that that was principally why he had fallen in with this idea of a fishing trip, so as to give Mother a little quiet. He said that young people seldom realize how much quiet means to people who are getting old. As to himself, he could still stand the racket, but he was glad to shelter Mother from it.

So we all drove away with three cheers for Mother, and Mother stood and watched us from the veranda for as long as she could see us, and

惜了。但她们俩都说，只要妈妈一句话，她们留在家里做事也很开心。我和威尔本来也可以不去的，但可惜做饭我们是一点忙也帮不上的。

因此，最后大家决定还是妈妈留在家里享受美好的一天，再做个晚饭。反正妈妈不喜欢钓鱼，再说虽然天气很好，阳光明媚，但外面还是有点凉飕飕的。爸爸很担心要是妈妈去了，可能会感冒。

他说妈妈原本可以好好休息休息的，可要是他拽着妈妈在乡下兜来兜去让她得了重感冒，他一辈子都不会原谅自己。他说，妈妈一直在为我们付出，因此尽量让妈妈休息休息，享受一下清净是我们大家的责任。爸爸还说，之所以想到去钓鱼主要就是想让妈妈清静清静。他说年轻人很少会明白清静对上了年纪的人多么重要。虽说吵点闹点他都还能受得了，但他要让妈妈享受清静。

于是我们大家欢呼着和妈妈告别后就开车走了。妈妈站在门廊那里，一直看着我们离开，直到再也看不到我

How We Kept Mother's Day

Father waved his hand back to her every few minutes till he hit his hand on the back edge of the car, and then said that he didn't think that Mother could see us any longer.

Well, we had the loveliest day up among the hills that you could possibly imagine, and Father caught such big fish that he felt sure that Mother couldn't have landed them anyway, if she had been fishing for them, and Will and I fished too, though we didn't get so many as Father, and the two girls met quite a lot of people that they knew as we drove along, and there were some young men friends of theirs that they met along the stream and talked to, and so we all had a splendid time.

It was quite late when we got back, nearly seven o'clock in the evening, but Mother had guessed that we would be late, so she had kept back the dinner so as to have it just nicely ready and hot for us[12]. Only first she had to get towels and soap for father and clean things for him to put on, because he always gets so messed up with fishing, and that kept Mother busy for a little while, that and helping the girls get ready.

But at last everything was ready, and we sat down to the grandest kind of dinner—roast turkey and all sorts of things like on X'mas day. Mother had to get up and down a good bit during the meal fetching things back and forward, but at the end Father noticed it and

们。爸爸不时往后向妈妈挥手,手都撞到后车身了才说妈妈应该已经看不到我们了。

不消说,可以想象我们在山上玩得多么开心啊,爸爸钓到几条老大的鱼,他说要是妈妈钓鱼,保准她怎么也拖不上来这些鱼。我和威尔也在钓鱼,不过我们没爸爸钓得多。姑娘们一路上遇见了很多熟人,她们在溪边还碰到几个朋友,都是年轻小伙子,他们相谈甚欢。所以大家都玩得开心极了。

我们回到家已经很晚了,差不多都晚上七点了。妈妈料到我们会晚归,就将晚餐推迟了。我们到家时晚饭刚做好,饭菜都热乎乎的呢。只是她还得先给爸爸拿来毛巾和肥皂,还有给他换洗的干净衣服,因为爸爸钓鱼总是弄得浑身很脏。此外她还帮姑娘们收拾停当,好一会才忙完。

一切总算忙妥当了,大家都坐下来吃饭。晚餐太丰盛了:烤火鸡,有各种各样的美食,和圣诞节吃的差不多。吃饭时,妈妈不停地起身、坐下,来回给大家传菜。快吃完时爸爸才注意到,他说妈妈完全不用这样,他要妈妈歇一歇。

said she simply mustn't do it, that he wanted her to spare herself, and he got up and fetched the walnuts over from the sideboard himself.

　　The dinner lasted a long while, and was great fun, and when it was over all of us wanted to help clear the things up and wash the dishes, only Mother said that she would really much rather do it, and so we let her, because we wanted just for once to humour her[13].

　　It was quite late when it was all over, and when we all kissed Mother before going to bed, she said it had been the most wonderful day in her life, and I think there were tears in her eyes. So we all felt awfully repaid for all we had done.

说着他起身亲自把对面餐柜里的核桃端了过来。

　　晚餐吃了好久，真是太开心了。吃完了，大家都想帮着收拾收拾，洗洗碗碟。可是妈妈说，她真的宁愿自己洗，于是我们都由着她，因为我们难得迁就她一次。

　　全部弄好后已经很晚了，上床睡觉前我们每个人都去吻了吻妈妈，妈妈说这今天是她这辈子最开心的一天，她眼中似乎还含着泪花。所以大家都觉得，我们为她做的一切真是太值得了！

▶ 注释：

1. take hold 的意思是"take root, become established"。母亲节是 1913 年才在美国设立的。根据前文，庆祝母亲节的倡议是近来提出的，因此按照原意译为"根深蒂固"不妥。在此，我们依据上下文，对其词义做适当的引申，可将其译为"接受，受欢迎"。

2. effort 一词在字典中的意思为"努力"，在此词义比较模糊，笼统地指母亲操持家务，照顾家人的所有事情。翻译时我们可以化虚为实，将其翻译为更加具体的词语如"精力"。注意虚实转换是一个较为常见的翻译技巧，使用得当，可以使译文意思表达更加明确。

3. 西方人过圣诞节时，有时会在纸上写上格言警句并装饰起来，将其放在壁炉上作为圣诞装饰的一部分。

4. four-in-hand tie 是指打平结的领带。平结是一种最简单的系领带的方式。在此不必译出。

5. remember sth. by "通过……记住"的意思。此处显然是指记住妈妈的为他们所付出的精力和感情。所以这里可以做适当的增补，译为"记住妈妈对他们的照顾和情意"。

6. 此句中 be going to 表示"打算"的意思应该翻译出来，而不是仅仅译出 be going to 所表达的"将来"之意。因为文中的家人都是说得多,做得少。他们在母亲节声称满足母亲的愿望,结果却是只满足了自己的愿望。

7. 根据上下文,这里的 said 是父亲解释为何要去钓鱼而不是兜风说的话,当然翻译成"说"也可以,但增补上语义中隐含有的"解释"二字,更准确一些。

8. so 表示结果。如果我们不加考虑,直接译为"于是"没有错,不过表现力不如"如此说来"。因为我们都觉得爸爸的说法挺好的,所以附和他。

9. 此处的 only 从上下文来看,是表示转折的意思,可译为"不过,只是"。

10. 查阅词典可知,stand in the way 是"阻碍,妨碍"之意。照搬词典含义,译文读起来很生硬。其实这里的"妨碍"就是指文中"我们"不要因为爸爸不能一起出游而感到内疚不安,而影响出游的兴致,故译者还是采用化虚为实的方法进行翻译。

11. 从原文来看,两姐妹遗憾的是在这么好的天气不能戴上新帽子出游而不是帮忙做饭。所以译者调整了一下词序,使译文语序更符合汉语表达的逻辑。

12. 原句较长,译为汉语时宜分拆为两个句子。

13. 按照词典可知,just for once:used to say that something unusual happens, especially when you wish it would happen more often(破例一次,难得一次)。humour:comply with other's wishes to keep them content.(遂人所愿而使其开心),故有此译。

(译注/唐毅)

On Poverty
论 贫 穷

By *Hilaire Belloc*

文/希拉里·贝洛克　译/唐毅

译者按: 希拉里·贝洛克(1870—1953),生于法国,长于英国,是一位多才多艺的诗人、散文作家和历史学家。贫穷是一个令人悲伤的话题,有谁愿意穷困一生呢?作者在此文中出人意料地论证贫穷给人带来的好处。作者没有引用贫穷锤炼人的意志等惯常的观点,而是一本正经地抛出并论证了如下几个观点:贫穷能使人慷慨;能让人丢掉幻想,面对现实;让人感恩,甚至能让穷人早点抵达地狱。作者观点鲜明,论证有力。作者娓娓道来,读者笑中带泪。笔触之间,颇见功力。翻译时,应注意传递作者看似严肃的语气,使之与表达的内容形成反差,从而传递出原文作者表达嘲讽的意图。

I had occasion the other day to give an address to a number of young men upon the matter of Poverty: which address I had intended to call "Poverty: The Attainment of It: the Retention of It When Attained." But I found that no explanation of my title was necessary. The young men knew all about it.

In giving this short address I discovered, as one always does in the course of speaking without

一天,我有机会给年轻人做个有关"贫穷"的演讲。我原定的题目是:贫穷——获得与保持。可是后来我发现无须解释,年轻人全都知道。

和脱稿演讲的人一样,在这个简短的演讲中,我也是讲着讲着才发现

On Poverty

notes, all manner of new aspects in the thing. The simple straightforward view of poverty we all know; how it is beneficial to the soul, what a training it is, how acceptable to the Higher Powers[1], and so on. We also know how all those men whom we are taught to admire began with poverty, and we all have, I hope, at the back of our minds a conception of poverty as a sort of foundation for virtue and right living.

But these ideas are general and vague. I was led by my discourse to consider the thing in detail, and to think out by reminiscence and reason certain small, solid, particular advantages in poverty, and also a sort of theory of maintenance in poverty: rules for remaining poor.

I thus discovered first of all a definition of poverty, which is this: Poverty is that state in which a man is perpetually anxious for the future of himself and his dependants, unable to pursue life upon a standard to which he was brought up, tempted both to subservience and to a sour revolt, and tending inexorably towards despair[2].

Such was the definition of poverty at which I arrived, and once arrived at, the good effects flowing from such a condition are very plain.

The first great good attendant upon poverty is that it makes men generous. You will notice that while some few of the rich are avaricious or mean, and while all of them have to be, from the very nature of their position, careful, the poor and

这个话题有各种新的方面可以探讨。对贫穷我们都有最简单、最直接的了解：它如何滋养人的灵魂，如何锤炼人，神灵怎样接受贫穷等等。我们也都知道，让我们仰慕的那些伟人曾经是怎样白手起家。我希望在我们每个人的潜意识里都有这样一个观念，即贫穷是培养美德和正确生活方式的基础。

但这只是一些笼统、不甚清晰的想法。在演讲过程中，我渐渐开始仔细思考。通过回忆和理性的分析，我给贫穷总结出几个小小的，但却是实实在在、独特的优点。同时我提出了所谓保持贫穷的理论，即保持贫穷的原则。

就这样，我首先发现了贫穷的定义，它是这样的：贫穷是一种状态。在此状态中，人总是为自己和家人的未来忧虑，无法追求他成长过程中曾经达到的一种生活标准，于是既想顺从又想反抗，最终不可避免地走向绝望。

这就是我给贫穷下的定义。一旦有了定义，贫穷的好处就显而易见了。

贫穷的第一大好处是它使人慷慨。你会发现不少富人或贪婪或吝啬，但所有富人因其地位所在都不得不小心而为。而生活窘迫的穷人，无论多穷，都很愿意分享他仅有的一切。

embarrassed man will easily share whatever little he has. True, this is from no good motive, but merely from a conviction that, whatever he does, it will be much the same in the end; so that his kindness to his fellows comes from a mixture of weakness and indifference. Still, it breeds a habit; and that is why men whose whole characters have been formed under this kind of poverty always throw away money when by any chance they get a lump of it.

  Then there is this other good attending poverty, that it cures one of illusions. The most irritating thing in the company of the rich, and especially of rich women, is the very morass of illusion in which they live. Indeed, it cannot be all illusion, there must be a good deal of conscious falsehood about it. But, at any rate, it is any abyss of unreality, communion with which at last becomes intolerable[3]. Now the poor man is physically[4] prevented from falling into such vices of the heart and intelligence. He cannot possibly think that the police are heroes, the judges superhuman beings, the motives of public men in general other than vile. He can nourish no fantasies upon the kind old family servant, or the captain of industry's supreme intelligence. The poor man is up against it, as the phrase goes. He is up against the bullying and corruption of the police, the inhuman stupidity of the captain of industry, the sly self-advancement of the lawyer, the abominable hypocrisies of the parasitical trades such as buttling. He comes across

诚然，这并非出自善意的动机，而是因为他们坚信，无论做什么，最终的结果都一样；因此，他善待同伴，既是因为贫穷弱势，也是因为无所谓的态度。尽管如此，贫穷还是培养出了分享这个好习惯。也正因为如此，在贫困中长大的人一旦得到一大笔钱，总是会肆意挥霍。

  其次，贫穷的另一大好处是它让人丢掉幻想。与富人相处，尤其是与贵妇人相处时，最恼人的是他们总是生活在各种各样的幻想中。其实，也并非所有都是幻想，大多还是她们有意自欺。但无论如何，这并非现实，一旦踏入这个深渊，最终都会变得难以忍受。然而，由于物质条件的限制，穷人不可能沾染这种心灵和智慧的恶习。他也不可能认为警察就是英雄，法官就是超人，公务人员一般不会心怀恶意，他亦不会对那些善良的老家仆，或是工业巨头的无敌精明心存幻想。正如老话所说，穷人四面楚歌。他会面临警察欺凌和腐败，受到毫无人性的工业巨头匪夷所思的压迫，被自抬身价的狡猾律师所欺骗，被令人作呕的、虚伪的寄生从业者如仆役侮辱。这一切遭遇，或亲历，或听闻，所以他不会视人世为乐园，正如士兵不会视战争如美景，水手不会视大海为

all these things by contact and the direct personal sensible experience. He can no more think of mankind as a garden than a soldier can think of war as a picture, or a sailor of the sea as a pleasure-place[5].

We may also thank poverty (those of us who are enjoying her favours) for cutting quite out of our lives certain extraordinary necessities which haunt our richer brethren. I know a rich man who is under compulsion to change his clothes at least twice a day, and often thrice, to travel at set periods to set places, and to see in rotation each of at least sixty people. He has less freedom than a schoolboy in school, or a soldier in a regiment; indeed, he has no real leisure at all, because so many things are thus necessary to him. But your poor man cannot even conceive what these necessities may be. If you were to tell him that he had to go and soak himself in the vulgarity of the Riviera for so many weeks, he would not understand the word "had" at all. He would say that perhaps there were some people who liked that kind of thing, but that anyone should do it without a strongly perverted appetite he would not understand.

And here's another boon of grinding, anxious, sordid poverty. There is no greater enemy of the soul than sloth; but in this state of ceaseless dull exasperation, like a kind of grumbling toothache, sloth is impossible. Yet another enemy of the soul is pride, and even the poor man cannot really nourish

游乐场一样。

我们（那些备受贫穷关照的人）也会感恩贫穷，因为它将许多生活所需从我们的生活中完全排除出去，而这些却是许多富裕弟兄们每日不可或缺的。我认识一位富人，他每天不得不至少更衣两次，常常是三次，每日定时定点地轮流去见至少60人，他还不如学校的学童、军队的士兵自由。其实，生活中必不可少的事情太多，反而享受不到一点乐趣。相反，穷人连这些必需品是什么都不明白。如果你告诉他必须到里维埃拉的海边去享受几周，他连为何是"必须"都无法明白。他会说，也许有人喜欢那样的享受。但是他无法理解，因为在他看来一个人没有非常非常强烈的欲望，是不会这样去享受。

贫穷让人煎熬，使人焦虑，悲惨兮兮，但还有一个好处。心灵最大的敌人莫过于懒惰。贫穷就像让人呻吟不已的牙痛一样，让人日复一日、不停地挣扎，因此人不可能懒惰。心灵的另一个敌人是骄傲，而穷人不可能真正

pride; he may wish to nourish it. Or, again, the inmost of man which an old superstition called "the Soul" is hurt by luxury. Now poverty, in the long run forbids or restricts luxury.

Poverty, I think, however, has a much nobler effect by the introduction of irony, which I take to be the salt in the feast of intelligence. I have, indeed, known rich men to possess irony native to themselves, so that it is like a picture which a man paints for his own pleasure and puts up on his own walls. All the poor of London have irony, and, indeed, poor men all over the world have irony; even poor gentlemen, after the age of fifty, discover veins of irony and are the better for them, as a man is better for sherry in his soup. Remark that irony kills stupid satire, and that to have an agent within one that kills stupid satire is to possess an antiseptic against the suppurative reactions of the mind.

Poverty, again, makes men appreciate reality. You may tell me that this is of no advantage. It is of no direct advantage, but I am sure it is of advantage in the long run, for if you ignore reality you will come sooner or later against it, like a ship against a rock in a fog, and you will suffer as the ship will suffer.

If you say to the rich man that some colleague of his has genius, he may admit it in a lazy but sincere of fashion. A poor man knows better; he may admit it with his lips, but he is not so foolish

滋生出骄傲来，即使他希望如此。还有一点，奢侈的生活对一个人的内心，就是迷信说法的"灵魂"，是有害的。而贫穷，终将禁止或限制一个人奢侈的可能。

然而，我认为贫穷如果加上自嘲，会有更好的结果。在我看来，自嘲是人之智慧盛宴的精髓。实际上，我知道富人天生就善于自嘲，如同一幅自娱之作，悬于自家之墙一样。伦敦的穷人善于自嘲，实际上全世界的穷人都是如此。那些囊中羞涩的君子，过了知天命之年才会自嘲，就像男人喜欢往汤里加点雪利酒，这并非坏事。有人说，自嘲比乏味的讥讽更有致命的杀伤力，若是一个人内心拥有这样的力量，那就拥有了能抵抗心灵腐败化脓的抗菌剂。

此外，贫穷还会使人珍惜现实。也许你会说贫穷并无裨益。但我认为，即使没有直接的裨益，但从长远来讲还是有益于人的。因为如果无视现实，你迟早会像迷雾中触礁被毁的船一样，碰得头破血流。

如果你对一个富人说，他的某个同事很有天才，他也许懒洋洋地承认，真心认为确实如此。而穷人却不傻，他也许嘴上承认，但不会蠢到真的

as to accept it.

Lastly, of poverty, I think this, that it prepares one very carefully for the grave. I heard it said once by a beggar in a passion that the rich took nothing with them down to death. In the literal acceptation of the text he was wrong, for the rich take down with them to death flattery, folly, illusion, pride and a good many lesser garments which have grown into their skins, and the tearing off of which at the great stripping[6] must hurt a good deal. But I know what this mendicant meant—he meant that they take nothing with them down to the grave in the way of motor-cars, hot water, clean change of clothes, and various intolerably boring games. The rich go down to death stripped of external things not grown into their skins; the poor go down to death stripped of everything. Therefore, in Charon's boat[7] they get forward, and are the first upon the further shore. And this, I suppose, is some sort of advantage.

相信。

我认为贫穷的最后一点好处是能精心地为一个人走向坟墓做着准备。我曾经听一个乞丐愤愤地说，富人死的时候，什么也带不走。从字面上来说他错了。因为富人离开人世的时候，带走了奉承、愚蠢、幻想、自傲和许多已入其骨、矫饰其人的恶习，因此在最后的涤罪洗过中，他们一定痛苦万分。但是我明白乞丐说这话的意思。他是说富人们不能将那些小汽车、热水、华服以及各种各样让人无法忍受的无聊至极的游戏带进坟墓。富人进入坟墓时带不走身外之物，而穷人一无所有地死去。因此，乘坐卡戎的小船前往地狱，穷人最先抵达。因此，我认为这也算是贫穷的某种好处吧。

注释：

1. 指掌握权力的神灵。

2. 此句较长，嵌套有多个定语从句，翻译时如果不做拆分，译文很难流畅。拆分是翻译定语从句时常用的方法。

3. 此处作者将非现实的想象比喻成一个深渊。译者将此暗喻分拆后翻译，使译文更流畅。

4. physically 表示"物质方面"之意。如果不将此副词拆分出来单独成句，译文读起来就会很别扭。

5. 这里的两个句子从语义上来说，存在因果关系。所以翻译时可以将它们合并为一个句子。同时为符合汉语的表达习惯,可以采用增补的方法,加上"所以"二字,将原文中隐含的因果关系表示出来。

6. 《神曲》中讲到灵魂升入天堂前要修炼忏悔,涤罪洗过。

7. 在古希腊神话中,Charon(卡戎)是冥界中用小船载鬼魂前往冥府的艄公。他不仅在冥河上摆渡,还肩负着分辨来到冥河岸边的是死者亡灵还是不应进入冥府的活人的任务,因此他也是分辨之神。在英语中,人们用习语 Charon's boat(卡戎的小船)来比喻人死后前往阴间的过程,相当于中文中的"黄泉路上"。

(译注/唐毅)

On Man's Extravagance
论 男 人 的 奢 侈

By J. B. Priestley

文/J. B. 普里斯特利　译/唐毅

译者按：普里斯特利(1894—1984)，英国剧作家、小说家、批评家。本文用诙谐的语言刻画了男人在消费时如何在同性面前一改往日做派，变得出手阔绰、豪气十足。翻译应尽量将作者叙述的语气如实地传达出来。

My friend C, the short-story writer, was telling us of some visit to the opera. He had gone in the company of another man, and had, it appeared, paid more for seats than he usually did. His wife broke in to chaff him because on the one occasion when she had not been with him he had paid more for the seats[1]. Then some one present remarked that it was strange, seeing that men generally spend most money when they are in the company of their womenfolk. "No," I said, with that air of finality, which has made me so universally disliked, "that is only a legend. Men are most extravagant in the company of other men." And, of course, I was right. They have

我的一位朋友是一名短篇小说家，他和我们讲起了某次看歌剧的经历。他和另一位男士同去，票好像比平日里买的贵一些。他妻子插话打趣他说，就这一次没跟着去，他就买了更贵的票。于是，在座的有一位就说这很奇怪，因为男人通常和女眷一起花钱最多。"非也，这只是传说。男人和男人在一起才最奢侈呢。"我武断地说道，这口气让我到哪儿都不招人待见。当然，我并没有说错。男人有时确实想在某个女人面前出出风头，但更多的时候还是和男人在一起时最奢侈。在这点上我认为男女大不一样。不过

their moments when they wish to dazzle some female or other, but by far the greater number of their really expensive moments occur when they are in the company of other men². In this respect they differ greatly from women, I think. I also think that all these generalizations about men and women are very wild. But though they are wild they are not necessarily false. They work, in the main, and they have the additional advantage of being entertaining.

Women may be economical or extravagant, parsimonious or spendthrift—and they usually err on one side or the other, very definitely—but whichever they are by nature, so they remain in all companies³. The presence of another woman does not disturb them at all. A mean woman remains mean, though her companion should shower money all over the place. Two women spending a day together, shopping, sightseeing, lunching and dining, theatre-going, and so forth, seem to act just as they would if they were each independent. They are not ashamed to keep a firm hand upon the purse-strings. And one may even see them carefully dividing the expenditure, handing one another six pences and shillings, or each paying her own bus fare. There has been no kind of economic coalition.

With men, however, it is very different. When two men spend some time together, lunching, dining, theatre-going, holiday-making, and so forth, there is formed, by some

我也感觉有关男人和女人的这些推论缺乏依据。但尽管如此，这些推论并不一定就是错的，它们大致在理，而且还颇为有趣。

女人或节俭，或奢侈，或吝啬小气，或大手大脚——而且可以肯定的是她们往往容易走极端。但是无论她们天生是什么样的性格，和谁在一起都是我行我素，绝不会因为身边多了个女伴而有所改变。吝啬的女人，即使同伴到处撒钱，她也依然吝啬。两个女人相处一天，一起购物观光，一起吃饭看戏，她们花钱的方式还是像独自一人时一样，彼此并不会受到对方的影响。她们并不羞于捏紧钱包。相反，你甚至还有可能看到她们仔细地分摊花销，你给我几便士，我给你几先令，或各付各的车费，女人之间绝无经济合作这种事。

可是，男人就完全不同了。两个男人若是在一起吃饭、看戏、度假什么的，就会莫名其妙地变成不同于其中任何一个的另一种人。这个"第三

On Man's Extravagance

mysterious process, a kind of person who is commonly different from either. He this third person, this mysterious spirit of the festive male, is the soul of generosity. He does not count the silver and pence. Money, as people say, is no object. He is always ready for "just another"; he only dines in the best restaurants and sits in the most expensive seats; he is a prince in disguise. Under the domination of this shadowy holiday captain, our two men each spend a great deal more than they would if they were alone. Even the very mean man desperately attempts at least to appear less mean. Neither of them dares to suggest economy, to hint at a prudent restraint, or even to suggest for a moment that there is such a thing as limiting one's expenditure[4]. When they are by themselves, a bus is sufficiently speedy and dignified mode of transport, but only a taxi will serve the coalition. A three-and-six penny dinner, a seat in the upper circle, a half-bottle of very modest Beaune, a nine-penny cigar, and so forth, will content the solitary masculine reveler[5], but let another join him and the dinner is trebled in price, the seats are stalls, the wine has a year attached to its name and is flanked by cock-tails and liqueurs, and the cigars are those by means of which companies are promoted and merged and dissolved, so that before they have done each man has probably spent at least three times his usual festive allowance.

Nor is it a matter of ordinary hospitality. We

者"男人莫名其妙地沉浸在欢庆节日的情绪中,简直就是豪爽的化身,他压根不管花多花少。正如人们说的那样,钱根本不是个事。他随时都会"再来一点"。他只在最好的餐厅用餐,只坐最贵的座位看戏:他简直就是乔装打扮的王子。于是在这个影子"节日队长"的撺掇下,我们的这两个男人各自都比独自一人时多花了许多。即使是非常吝啬的男人,至少也会尽力表现得不那么吝啬。他们谁都不敢提议节约,谁都不敢暗示要精打细算,甚至从来不提什么限制花销。虽然他们独自一人时,乘公共汽车就够快够体面了,但若是一帮男人在一起,那就非出租车不可了。三四英镑的一顿晚餐,剧院楼厅的座位,半瓶价钱不贵的伯恩红酒,九便士的雪茄之类的,就会让一个独自找乐的男人心满意足。但如果再来一个男人,那么晚餐就得花三倍的钱,座位得是正厅的前排,葡萄酒得是标了年份的,而且还得和鸡尾酒、利口酒(餐后甜酒)一块儿端上来,雪茄得是公司搞营销、谈兼并议拆分时用的那种上等雪茄。如此一来,饭局还没开始,很可能各人的花费都已至少三倍于通常的节日用度了。

而这个还不是普通的请客招待。

are not describing one man entertaining another, playing the lavish host, but two (or three or four) men merely spending the day or the evening together. It is true that what actually happens is that both men entertain one another, alternately playing host. But it is the presence of the intangible but very real third man, this festive spirit evoked when our two men come together, that makes the difference. He it is who blows away, with one contemptuous breath, the customary scale of expenditure, and puts in its place what we might call the "coalition" scale, which demands the best of everything and always "just another" some thing or other[6]. This spirit is not evoked when male goes out with female. At certain seasons, when mating is in the air and the male seeks to dazzle, to astonish, to take by storm and to capture, he may be extravagant enough, emptying his pocket in the lordliest fashion under her bright eyes, but this is only one of the whimsies of the mating season. The mood does not last. A man often spends a good deal of money when a woman accompanies him because he knows that, though she may protest, she will be secretly delighted, admiring his magnificence, and because he enjoys her pleasure (the half of woman's charm) in the host of little extravagances[7]. This being so, he is spending money to some purpose, buying something that is worth every farthing of the price asked for it, for what he is doing but brightening the loveliest eyes, flooding with colour the softest cheeks, and

这里并不是说男人请客做东而出手大方，而是说两个(或三四个)男人只是在一起消磨一天或一个晚上的情况。虽然实际情况通常是大家轮流请客，但正是这看不见却又非常真切的"第三人"的存在，正是这种两个男人在一起时才有的过节的心情，才使情况变得不同。他对习以为常的消费水平嗤之以鼻，取而代之的，我们或可称其为"合作"消费水平，也就是他什么都要最好的，总是在说"再来一点"这个或那个。男人和女人外出就不会产生这种情绪。在空气中充满了男欢女爱气息的某些季节，男人想要在女人面前大出风头、想一举征服她时，他或许就会挥霍一把。在她明眸的注视下，派头十足地掏空自己的钱包。但这不过是恋爱时期的荒唐行为，这种情绪并不能持久。男人在女人面前出手阔绰，往往出于两个原因。一是他深谙女人之心，知道虽然她嘴上反对，心里却暗自窃喜，欣赏他的豪爽大方；二是他也喜欢看到女人因他时不时地来点小小的奢侈而高兴（女人一半的魅力就在于此）。因此他这是钱尽其用，买得物有所值。他做的一切不就是为了让那可爱的眼睛更加明亮，让那娇嫩的双颊更加艳丽，让世上那最美的柔唇泛起一抹笑颜吗？这钱花得太值了，简直就是一笔好的投资。

curling into a smile the most beautiful mouth in the world[8]? This is money well spent, simply a sound investment.

But with another man, there is no question of taking pleasure in the spectacle of the other's happiness[9]. The two revelers are either slaves of some queer unwritten convention or are being enchanted. The extra money they spend is not soundly invested but is simply conjured out of their pockets. When they have shaken hands, slapped backs and roared and guffawed together for a few minutes, the spell begins to work. Their two personalities contrive to create this other being, the grand, careless prince of men about town. Once he takes charge, passbooks fade into the distance, the taxes are an old unhappy dream, rent and school-fees and the last installment for the car all vanish and leave no trace behind them, and the world is their oyster[10]. With a few kingly gestures he conjures out of their pocket-cases all the notes that have been lying there, snugly awaiting the next domestic financial crisis. I do not know if this mysterious creature has a name, for he certainly can be evoked without any name being pronounced. But I suspect that his title is "Dash-it-all"[11]. I suspect this because I have noticed that when our revelers have warmed to the work and are trampling economy underfoot, it is this title that comes most often to the lips. Flushed and hot eyed, under the spell of this enchanter, at every new stop they pronounce his name. "Dash-it

但是男人和同性在一起，就不可能从对方的快乐中获得快感。两个男人一起找乐子，如果不是迫于某种不成文的奇怪传统，那就是中了邪了。额外支出的钱不是一笔好的投资，而是像被施了魔法似的从他口袋里跑出来的。两人勾肩搭背，扯着嗓子又说又笑，不一会魔咒就开始发挥作用了。两个男人的个性共同造就了这个"他者"，造就了这个花钱豪爽、满不在乎的公子哥儿。一旦他占了上风，于是乎存折被抛到了脑后，交税不过是旧日的梦魇，什么房租、学费、最后一期的汽车贷款什么的全都消失得无影无踪，从此他尽可随心所欲。只消几个王者般潇洒的动作，他便变戏法似地掏光了口袋里的那几张钞票，然后就老老实实地等待家里下一次经济危机的到来。我不知道这个神秘的"他者"是否有专门的称谓，但显然并没有人叫过他的名字，他就不请自来了。然而我还是怀疑他的名字叫"去他的"。我这般怀疑是因为我发现每当作乐者一来劲就把节俭忘得一干二净的时候，他的口头禅就是这样。在这位魔法师的魔咒下，男人们玩得脸面泛光，两眼发红，每到一个新的地方都会这样说。"去他的，"一个说，"我们不如去克罗伊斯饭店大撮一顿！""去他的，"另一

all," one of them cries, "we might as well dine at the Croesus, where we can get a decent feed." "Dash-it-all," cries the other, "we might as well order two bottles." Then after they have dash-it-alled[12] through eight-year-old brandy and very large Coronas, one of them will say, "Dash-it-all! We might as well finish up at the Rotunda." And Dash-it-all whispers that it might as well be a box. Great is Dash-it-all!

个嚷嚷道,"我们不妨再要两瓶酒。"于是,等他们一边喊着"去他的",一边干完八年陈的白兰地,抽完大号的上等日冕雪茄,又有人会说,"去他的!我们再上圆形大剧院去!"然后,这个"去他的"又嘀咕说,那就来个包厢吧。啊,"去他的"真是太棒了!

注释:

1. 此句 because 没有直接译作"因为",而是用"说"一字引出这个原因,这样表达更加通顺。还应注意的是 the one occasion 这个短语的确切含义。通过查词典可以发现,one 还有"唯一"的意思,故翻译为"就这一次",符合上下文的意思。

2. 这里 by far 修饰比较级,强调程度,此处的意思是"多得多"。注意不要和 so far 混淆,后者是"迄今为止"的意思。

3. to err on the side of sth. 是一个惯用语,它的意思是 to be more careful or safe than is necessary, in order to make sure that nothing bad happens,由此我们可以理解,有的女人宁可过于节约,有的女人则宁可过于奢侈,用一个简单的词语来形容就是"容易走极端"。

4. 这个句子较长,造成 suggest for a moment 不容易理解。但是如果注意到句首的否定词 neither,就不难理解这里是 not for a moment(从来不曾)的意思。

5. 此句没有将原文的 three-and-six penny 直译成"三英镑六便士",主要是因为这里的数词其实是虚指,因此译者将其改成了"三四英镑",以符合中文读者的阅读习惯。另外注意 modest 一词的用法,《英汉大词典》里 modest 的第四个义项是:"不太大(或多)的,不过分的,适中的,适度的",而从原文的语义来看,这里似乎在讲不用花很多钱的意思,为了弄清确切的词义,我们不妨多查几本词典,最好还要查阅原版词典。朗文词典里给出的释义中,有一条便是:not very great, big or expensive。因此可以确定,这里应该译为"价钱不贵的"。

6. 这里用了比喻的修辞手法。翻译时遇到比喻,一种办法是直译,这自然最省事。但实际上并非所有比喻都能直译,很多时候照搬过来转译成目的语有种怪怪的味道。比如这句话直译过来是:用鄙夷的口气,吹走了惯常的消费水平。这个比喻显然不符合我们汉语的习惯。这时就得先理解透原文,再将其转换成符合目的语习惯的语言。

7. 此句不仅长,而且复杂,包含了一个时间状语从句和两个原因状语从句,其中第一个原因状语从句里还包含了一个宾语从句和一个让步状语从句。这是英语里常见的长句,也是英语不同于汉语的一个特点。如果按照原句结构译成汉语,不免显得冗长烦琐,因此译者在翻译过程中动了一番脑筋,首先点明男人出手阔绰有两个原因,然后分别道出这两个原因是什么。这样译文不仅清楚易懂,而且读起来也更加流畅。另外句中的 the host of little extravagances(许多小小的奢侈;host of:large number of)是一个名词短语,如果将其译成动词短语"时不时或经常来点小小的奢侈",可以使句子更加符合汉语的表达习惯。此处我们将"许多"所包含的频度含义转化成"时不时"。

8. spending money to some purpose:花得有意义,花到点子上;句子用了进行时,含有"他这么做"的意思,所以加了"这是"。注意,一个句子所用的时态不同,表达的含义也会不同。另外,but 后面并列的三个词组也整齐地放在"不就是为了"之后,保留了原文的排比结构,原文肯定句的语气在译文中也变为反问句,这样原文结构和语气都原汁原味地体现了出来。

9. 英语中常有一词多义的现象,翻译时要根据上下文确定词语的意思。there is no question of 在《英汉大词典》里有两个意思,"……是毫无疑问的"和"……是不可能的"。这是两个截然相反的意思,究竟取哪个含义就要我们根据上下文来确定了。上文提到男人在某个女子面前大手大脚地花钱是想取悦她,在同性面前他们也"毫无疑问"地这样做吗?从下一句来看显然不是的,因此可以确定,这里的 There is no question of 应该取第二个意思,否则前后意思就衔接不上了。

10. 注意这里的 take charge 是英语里的常用搭配,是"负责"的意思,虽然上下文说的是钱的问题,charge 也有"费用,价钱"的意思,但这里的 charge 与钱无关。World is his oyster 是一个习语,意思是 there is no limit to the opportunities that someone has,这里结合上下文,将其译成了"随心所欲"。

11. dash-it-all 是个委婉的诅咒语,文中指男人准备花钱时的一个口头禅,考虑到作者又将其作为花钱豪爽的"第三者"的名字,这里将其译成"去他的",两者兼顾。

12. 此句中的 dash-it-all 是作者自己造的一个动词。译者结合情景将 dash-it-all through 译为"一边喊着'去他的',一边……",比较妥帖。

(译注/唐毅)

The Wife
妻　子

By *H. V. Morton*

文/H. V. 莫顿　　译/唐毅

译者按：莫顿(1892—1979)，英国记者、游记作家。本文用幽默的语言描写了普通家庭夫妻之间的关系。当新婚的热情褪去，生活渐渐平淡下来后，丈夫变得麻木了，对妻子产生了不满，而妻子面对丈夫的冷淡也心有不甘。作者用生动的语言将夫妻之间的这种微妙关系刻画得栩栩如生。翻译时尤其要注意男女之间对话的语气。

The ordinary wife lives in an ordinary home, sometimes with an extraordinary husband, who, in his heart of hearts, thinks she has an easy time. Can she not stay at home when he is forced unwillingly to meet the rain of a summer morning in perpetual pursuit of money?[1] Compared with his complicated life her little problems are purely childish.

If he is one of those "homey" men who love to potter and snoop about the house like an amateur plumber, he secretly envies her. How happy he would be if he could stay at home all

寻常人妻生活在寻常人家，有时也会有一个不寻常的丈夫。在丈夫的心中，妻子的日子过得很轻松。在夏日的早晨，当他万般不愿地冒雨出门，马不停蹄地去挣钱时，她可以不在家里待着吗？与他复杂的生活相比，她的那些小问题真是太小儿科了。

若他是那种居家男人，喜欢像业余的水管工那样在家东捣捣西捣捣，他会暗自羡慕她。要是他也能整天待在家里，开心地随便捣鼓，该多好啊！若他是一个硬汉

day and just muddle around delightfully. If he is a sterner type he likes to think of the ease and comfort which his strenuous efforts have brought to the woman of, I was going to say, his choice.

In accordance with the romantic English custom she is penniless, and therefore at his mercy. If he turns out a bad lot she is tied to him by pride, necessity, or children[2]. Sometimes he is amused to observe her working up prettily to a request for money. Instead of saying, "You need a new costume and I would like you to have it," he waits for her to sit on the arm of his chair and wheedle round him:

"I wonder if you could let me have a cheque…"

"What for?"

"I haven't had anything new for ages."

"But that thing you've got on is beautiful. Surely you don't need a new one yet!"

"Surely you don't need a new one yet!" how can he know that she has fallen in love with a dress in a shop-window as fiercely as a boy with a steam engine; that she hardly dares to look in the window in case some other woman has taken that dress[3].

It seldom occurs to him, unless he is an unusual type, that it is humiliating for her to beg; he does not attempt to save her from it; in fact, he rather likes it; it makes him feel generous and powerful.

子，他总是会想自己怎样拼命努力为他的女人，我是说为他心爱的女人，带来了舒适和安逸的生活。

依照浪漫的英国传统，妻子身无分文，凡事都听命于丈夫。就算到头来发现丈夫是个坏蛋，妻子还是会或出于自尊、或迫不得已、或为了孩子继续和他生活在一起。丈夫有时看着妻子怀揣小心思，一步一步地开口问他要钱时的样子，他就很开心。他不会主动说，"你需要买新衣服啦，我想让你有新衣服穿"，而是等着她坐到他椅子的扶手上讨好地说：

"我想，你是不是可以给我一张支票呢……"

"干什么用啊？"

"人家好久没买新衣服了嘛。"

"可你现在穿的就很漂亮啊！还要买什么新衣服啊！"

"还要买什么新衣服！"他哪里知道她看中了商店橱窗里的一条裙子，就像小男孩痴迷蒸汽机一样；他哪里知道她都几乎不敢往那橱窗里看，生怕那条裙子已被其他女人买走了。

丈夫若非特别之人，他很少想到妻子开口求他是一种屈辱，而且他才不会想要去改变呢。其实他倒还乐在其中，因为这使他觉得自己慷慨大方，权力在握。

In the sharp, temperamental clashes, for which small houses are designed, he sometimes thinks that he has made a bad bargain—that all men make bad bargains. Surely, he thinks, some wives try to become proficient at their jobs. It is true that her early life was devoted to the arts and not to the stern practicalities of an unpaid profession (But surely not unpaid? Is he not the reward?). She was taught to play the piano badly and to sing sickly ballads and to paint messy water-colours, achievements which served their purpose and invested her in those romantic days with a spurious halo of cleverness.

He thinks in dyspeptic moments, as the shoulders of sheep and the ribs of bulls follow one another across his table in dull and unimaginative[4] procession, that were he a wife he would have set himself to learn the profession of housekeeping from A to Z. He would have become the best housekeeper on earth[5].

He would have studied cookery and have invented dishes. He would have invented all kinds of things. He would have surrounded himself with proficient and obedient servants ("Of course, they can be found!") who would leap respectfully to his orders instead of pottering round in slipshod revolt.

After all, what is there to manage in a small house?

当夫妻性格不合发生激烈争吵时——斗室之家莫不如此，他有时会感觉自己做了一桩亏本的买卖——他认为男人都吃亏。在他看来，当然也有一些人妻会努力去胜任自己的工作。确实，她的早年生活都献给了艺术，哪是这种毫无报酬的破事儿（但真的没有报酬吗？丈夫难道不是妻子得到的回报吗？）。她学会了弹个蹩脚的钢琴，唱点难听的民谣，画点涂鸦一样乱七八糟的水粉画。这些才艺也曾发挥过作用，让她在谈情说爱那会儿戴了个"聪明伶俐"的虚假光环。

在他心情不好的时候，看着一道道羊肩肉、牛肋骨这些毫无新意、司空见惯的菜端到桌上，他就会想，要是换成他是妻子，一定会从头到尾好好学习如何操持家务，说不定他早就是世界上最好的主妇了。

他会精心研究厨艺，发明新菜，各种各样的新菜。他的身边会围着称职又听话的仆人，他们都毕恭毕敬、随时听命于他（不消说，一定找得到这样的仆人！），而不是懒洋洋地混日子来消极抵抗。

毕竟，就一间小小的房子，有啥好管理的呢？

The Wife

She, having long ago descended from the hills of romance into the deeper but less exciting valleys of affection, finds herself surrounded, swamped, smothered, and obsessed by the trivial[6]. At the back of her mind is the mournful reflection that had she not been so surrounded, swamped, smothered, and obsessed she might have been vaguely brilliant at—what? That is not clear.

In her moments of dyspepsia she feels shut up in a box. There is no escape[7]. The wide, thrilling world goes on outside and she is cooped up with an unwilling girl, tied to perpetual problems[8] concerning the buying of minute quantities of milk, bread, meat, and vegetables.

Her life is a stupid routine of ordering dust to be removed from rooms designed to hold as much dust as possible; of ordering the minute portions of food to be cooked; of seeing that the plates which contained the food are washed up; distressing trivialities which go on three times a day year after year[9]. She is the slave of cleanliness, cookery, and monotony. She knows that she is an amateur, but she does her best with shocking bad material and little money; she knows that she is no organizer; but she does not realize that she is one of[10] millions of similar amateurs who support, instead of combining to abolish, the stupid tyranny of the kitchen. Some day a wife will press a button

而妻子，早就从浪漫之爱的山上，下到了更加平淡的爱的深谷。她发现自己被鸡毛蒜皮的家务琐事所困，深陷其中，无法自拔，这些琐事压得她喘不过气来。她在心里也会哀怨，要不是这样被家务琐事缠得喘不过气来，无法脱身，或许她早已有所成就了呢——什么成就呢？那就不清楚了。

妻子在心情抑郁的时候，则会觉得自己身陷笼中，无处可逃。外面的世界那么辽阔，那么精彩刺激，而她却和一个不听话的小女仆守在一起，总也有做不完的事儿，一会儿要去买点牛奶面包，一会儿又要去买肉和蔬菜，简直没完没了。

她的生活就是一堆一成不变的破事儿：本来就只等着积灰的房间，要叫人打扫干净；一点点餐食，要吩咐下去煮好；盛过食物的餐盘，要盯着人洗好。日复一日、年复一年都是这些琐碎家务，令她烦恼不堪。每天打扫卫生、烧饭备餐，生活单调乏味。她知道自己只是个业余的"管家"，但是在食材差、钱又少的情况下她还是尽力而为；她知道自己根本不擅长组织领导，但她也没有意识到除她之外还有千万个有相同处境的业余"管家"，她们非但没有联合起来推翻这种荒唐的"厨房暴政"，反而成了它的帮凶。终有一天为人妻者可以按一下按钮，食物就会飞快地从公共厨房送过来；再按

75

and food will shoot in from a communal kitchen; she will press another and the remnants of the feast will disappear.

It is only the capacity which women have for suffering in silence and their instinctive inability to combine which have preserved the stupidities of the kitchen.

She can sense every mood of her husband[11]. She knows at once when he is laboriously carrying a secret; when he is clumsily trying to hide anything[12]. He, on the other hand, is blind to those occasions when, watching him sitting so placidly after his exciting day, she longs to utter a loud scream and hit his bald head with the nearest metal implement. She wishes at times that he was less fond of his home. He is becoming part of the unadventurous routine. Is there no excitement in life; no unexpectedness? It is also the anniversary of their wedding. He has forgotten[13]. She says to him hopefully:

"George, what day is it to-day?"

"Thursday," he replies promptly, looking over the evening paper.

"Hullo," he adds, "what's up?"

"Don't speak to me!" she cries, and bursts into tears; which pains and horrifies him. An entirely comfortable world has been suddenly shattered for no reason whatsoever![14] In a moment of accidental inspiration he suggests a dinner and a theatre. In the taxicab on the way

一下按钮,丰盛大餐的残羹剩饭就会消失不见。

厨房里的荒唐传统之所以得以维持下来,就是因为女性总是能够默默忍耐痛苦,因为她们天生缺乏团结合作的能力。

妻子对丈夫的情绪明察秋毫。如果丈夫正费力地守着一个秘密,她立马就知道;如果他笨手笨脚地想要隐藏什么,她也一看便知。可他呢,压根不知道有时候自己忙碌了一天之后,妻子看着他心安理得地坐在一边时,恨不得大叫一声,顺手操起手边的金属工具砸向他那光秃秃的脑袋。还有些时候她真希望丈夫不要这么喜欢自己的家,因为他也渐渐变成了她日常琐事的一部分,平淡无奇。生活难道不再令人激动?不再有意外的期待?那天还是他们的结婚纪念日,可他却忘记了。于是她满心期待地问道:

"乔治,今天是什么日子呀?"

"星期四啊,"他马上答道,眼睛还看着晚报。

"喂,怎么了?"他接着问道。

"不跟你说了!"她大叫着哭了起来。看到她哭,他又烦又怕。好端端的世界瞬间就这样无缘无故地毁了!他灵机一动,随口说咱们出去吃顿饭,再去看场戏吧。回家的路上,坐在出租车里,觉得妻子看起来挺漂亮的,就亲了

back he thinks she looks rather brilliant. He kisses her, feeling slightly foolish. She responds with great enthusiasm. She is like something escaped. Later, when screwing his neck round to battle with his starched collar, he says:

"We must… damn this stud … go out a bit more… oh, confound the thing!"

"Do you love me?" she asks with alarming earnestness.

"You know I do. Good Lord—what's the matter now?"[15]

"Oh, nothing, only I'm so—I can't help it—happy!"

(Women, so think these excellent husbands, are really *most extraordinary*.)

她一下,感觉自己有点傻傻的。可她却像是一下子从哪里挣脱了出来似的,热烈地回吻了上来。后来,他一边扭着脖子想解开浆洗得硬邦邦的衣领,一边说:

"我们得……这可恶的纽扣,多出来走走……哦,这该死的扣子!"

"你爱我吗?"她问道,语气认真得让人心里发慌。

"还用说吗?天啊,又怎么啦?"

"哦,没什么,我只是……只是太开心了,忍不住要问问嘛!"

(女人啊,这些优秀的丈夫想,真是太不寻常了。)

✦ 注释:

1. 此处不能将 can she not stay 理解为等同于 can't she stay,后者的意思是"难道她不能",而这里的意思是他嫉妒妻子可以在家待着,因此译为"她可以不……吗?"

2. turn out to be a bad guy,有"没想到他是这样的人"的意思,这里不宜译成"原本……"。

3. in case:她不敢看是怕衣服被买走了而心里难受。分号后面是 that,所以这个分句也是前面 know 的宾语,妻子的这种心理丈夫并不知道,因此译文用了两个"哪里知道",原汁原味地体现了原文的语气。

4. 这里的 dull 和 unimaginative 看起来是修饰 procession,其实不然。这两个词是转移修饰词,修饰前面提到的羊肩和牛肋骨。因为从上下文中我们可以得知,丈夫对妻子的厨艺不满意,而不是对菜端上来餐桌的方式不满意。

5. 注意表达 that 从句的虚拟语气。

6. 作者用了两个暗喻 hills 和 valleys 来比喻婚姻从激情走向平淡。翻译时要注意将此修辞手法翻译出来。此外,原句较长,宜如译文一样,根据语义做断句处理。

7. 原文两个句子语义紧密相连，所以翻译时将其合并为一个句子，使语义表达更加紧凑。

8. 此处的 perpetual problem 指的是后面买牛奶、蔬菜等。tied to 原意是"被……所困住"，此处采取反译的方法将其译为"总也有做不完的事儿"。此外，还依据 perpetual 一词，在句末加上"简直没完没了"进行增补，在不改变原文意思的前提下加强译文的表现力。

9. 原句较长，routine 一词后接了三个 of 短语，翻译时注意这三个并列的介词短语，保持并列成分的句式基本一致。另外，根据汉语表达习惯，对句子进行拆分断句，将原来的一个句子译为两个句子。前一个句子先概括她的生活，然后列举具体的家务琐事。后一个句子总结她做家务的感受。断句后，意思没有发生改变，但是句子的语义层次表达得更加清楚了。

10. one of 没有译成"……之一"，而是根据语义按照汉语习惯译成"除……之外还有千万个……"，用"还有"一词表达出她也是其中之一的意思，这样避免了较为欧化的表达，更符合汉语习惯。

11. 此处译者适当发挥移入语的优势，将妻子了解丈夫情绪的每一种变化用"明察秋毫"来表示，意思未变，但表现力更佳。

12. 原文一个主句后接了两个从句。译文为了使句子更加平衡，增补了"她也一看便知"。

13. 根据语义，将这两个句子进行合并，使语义表达更加紧凑。

14. don't speak to me 直译过来就是"不要和我说话"，但是作者想要表达的是女子生气了，不想和丈夫继续对话，从语用角度来看，这时女子一般会说"不跟你说了"。原文后半部分用了一个非限制性定语从句，译者将其单独成句，保留了原文的含义，又使译文更加符合汉语习惯。注意，定语从句并非一定要作为定语来翻译，尤其是非限制性定语从句。

15. 此句中的 now 虽是"现在"，what's the matter now 直译过来是"现在怎么了"，但是这句话显然不符合汉语习惯。其实从上下文中可以看出，此时男人因为妻子一会儿这样一会儿那样而有些忐忑不安，因此可以理解为"这下又怎么了？"从词典可以查到，"what is it now" is used when you are annoyed because someone keeps interrupting you or asking you things，此处同理。

（译注/唐毅）

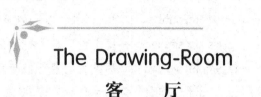

The Drawing-Room
客　厅

By *Mary Elizabath Coleridge*
文/玛丽·伊丽莎白·柯勒律治　译/唐毅

译者按：玛丽·伊丽莎白·柯勒律治(1861—1907)，英国小说家、诗人。《客厅》一文用平实的文字回忆了童年时期客厅留给她的美好印象，以及在她心中的地位。在作者眼里，客厅是温暖的，是充满快乐的，是她游戏的乐园。文章之所以能够引起共鸣，是因为我们每个人对自己童年生活过的地方都会有相似的记忆。翻译时需把握好平实的语气，将作者的美好情感真实地再现出来。

I sometimes wonder how the room I sit in looks to other eyes.

"Do you live in London all the year round?" people say; and then, even if they are too civil to condole, their eyes take a compassionate expression[1]. Alas, how that good thing, pity, is wasted! Who would be so lavish of love or of money? Once—once only I think—it happened to me to be envied. "You people who live in London do not know how glorious it is. You cannot!" said a British Resident in Foreign Parts, whose drawing-room

有时我会想，我坐着的这个客厅，别人是怎么看的呢？

"你常年都住伦敦吗？"人们问我。即使他们出于礼节嘴上不说同情我的话，眼中也会带着同情的目光。唉，这份美好的同情心就这样白白浪费了！有谁愿意这样滥施爱心和钱财呢？我也曾被人羡慕过——我想那是唯一的一次。"你们这些住在伦敦的人，哪里感受得到伦敦有多好呢，你们不可能体会到的！"一位侨居国外的英国公使这样说道。她家的客厅是一片丛林。

was a jungle.

To have lived in one place ever since memory began is to have seen that place change as you change yourself; but more perceptibly. Our own faces and figures in a glass are strange to us as the forms of those with whom we are not acquainted. I do not know after what fashion the little girl who played battledore and shuttle-cock here differed from the big girl who came after her, and the woman who now sits in her place. But I know that long ago the drawing-room was much larger than it is now, all the chairs and tables much higher, and the piano unaccountably higher still. It was a vast space of country in those days. I owned a little of it here and there—a dusty cabinet in the backwoods where my story-books lived—and everything underneath the piano. The rest had nothing to do with me[2]. The beautiful brick[3] towers almost as high as myself that I built upon that alien territory were doomed to fall, a few minutes after they were finished. I grieved for them. It seemed to me that they adorned the drawing-room.

In the firelight, of a winter's evening, my possessions expanded. As I danced in and out of the wreaths of white roses on the faded crimson ground of the carpet, I thought those also were mine. And if I had a cold, the sofa belonged to me.

After that came a dreadful time, when I

打记事起就住在一个地方,意味着你目睹了这个地方随着你的成长变化而变化,而且你对它的变化感受更深。我们在镜中看到自己的面孔和身形,陌生得如同那是我们素不相识的人。我不知道,当年那个玩板羽球、踢毽子的小女孩和后来的那个大姑娘,还有现在这个坐在她位置上的女子有何不同。但我知道,很久以前,客厅比现在大,桌椅都比现在高,而且不知何故,钢琴更是比现在高。那时候,客厅就像一片辽阔的国土,这儿或那儿我都拥有小小的一席之地——比如偏安于客厅一隅的落满灰尘的柜子,那是我故事书的栖身之地——还有钢琴下面也都是我的地盘。其他地方便没有我的份了。我在那片异国领土上搭的漂亮积木塔,差不多有我一人高,搭好不一会就倒塌。我很心痛,因为我觉得它们可使客厅增色不少呢。

冬日傍晚,熊熊炉火中,属于我的东西就多了一些。客厅里铺着褪了色的深红色地毯,我在上面的白玫瑰花环图案上跳进跳出。此时便觉得这一切都是属于我的。要是感冒了,沙发也属于我了。

后来我几乎完全被关在了客厅外面,

was shut out of the drawing-room almost entirely[4]. An exile feels as I used to feel when I passed the door[5]. Within there was quiet, peace, music, and books to read that were never dull. Without—sums, scales, French verbs, and everything that make existence dreary[6]. Even if I did get in, I was turned out remorselessly when a particular clock struck, and whenever people began to say something I should like to have heard[7].

By-and-by, when there were parties, I was brought down to sit with a book behind the piano. Thus I made the acquaintance of *King Lear* and was not greatly horrified. Thence I witnessed a love-scene for the first time. My aunt called me away, afraid lest my too evident sympathy should interrupt it.

A little later on, I came to view the drawing-room in the light of a Theatre[8]. There did I appear, first as the Beasts in a black mask, then as the radiant red velvet Prince, wedding his Beauty—I did enact Theseus[9]—I was a wandering Duchess—I was a Puritan in red ancestral boots. The drawing-room was musical with sweet voices then—full of people coming and going. Once I remember that we danced there.

As I sit alone, I wonder who will come when I also have gone.

I should like to think of another child—merrier—not so much afraid of the dark on the

这段时间简直糟糕透了。当我经过客厅门前时,感觉自己像是被流放了。厅内安静祥和,有音乐,有书籍,从来都不会感觉无聊;厅外却是算术、比例尺、法语动词,全都是让生活索然无味的东西。即使我好不容易进了客厅,什么时候到点的钟声一响,什么时候他们要谈个我也想听的话题,我就会被无情地赶出去。

不久,家里有聚会的时候,我被带到楼下,手捧一本书坐在钢琴后面。就这样,我开始第一次读《李尔王》,并没有感到十分害怕。在那里,我第一次目睹了有人在亲热。阿姨马上叫我走开,唯恐我过于明显的同情搅了他们的好事。

再往后,我开始将客厅当作伦敦大剧院。在那里,我演过头戴黑色面具的野兽,后来野兽变身为穿着红丝绒礼服、容光焕发的王子,和他的美女在举行婚礼——我演过特修斯——演过流浪的公爵夫人——我穿着祖传红靴子扮演清教徒。那时,客厅里有美妙的音乐,有甜美的歌声,那里宾客满堂,川流不息。记得我们还曾在那里跳过一场舞。

独自坐在这里,不知道我离开之后,有谁将会来到这里。

我想,应该还会有个小孩子吧——比我活泼,也不像我这样害怕外面黑黑

stairs outside—and that her mother would play and sing. I should like to think of another girl— as gay, as full of bold ambition and not so shy—acting and dancing where I danced and acted. I hope she will see the greatest man in the world come in, as I saw Robert Browning[10] come through the door one evening, his hat under his arm. I wonder whether she will train the creeper over the balcony to the west and plant geranium and mignonette, and sit there in summer to watch the gild of sunset over the roofs. Bright be her pictures in that shining window, and may she sometimes love a book that I loved[11].

的楼梯——她妈妈会边弹边唱。我想应该还会有个小女孩在我曾经跳过舞和表演过的地方演着戏，跳着舞——她和我一样快乐，一样雄心勃勃，但没有这么害羞。希望她能像我有一天晚上看到罗伯特·布朗宁腋下夹着一顶帽子从门外进来那样，看到举世伟人迈步进来。我不知道她是否会牵引攀缘植物越过阳台到西边生长，是否会种下天竺葵和木犀草，是否会在夏日坐在那里端详屋顶上的金色夕阳。愿她的身影在那洒满阳光的窗户里明媚如画，愿她偶尔也会爱上一本我爱过的书。

▶ 注释：

1. too... to do something 的意思是"太……以至于不能做某事"，直译过来便是"太有礼貌了，以至于没有表示同情"，但是直译显然不符合中文的表达习惯。

2. had nothing to do with me 的意思是"与我无关"，但是此处若译为"与我无关"让人觉得"我"对其他地方不感兴趣，从下文来看应该是"我"对其他地方没有做主的权利，故译者认为将其译为"没有我的份"更加确切。

3. brick 的意思除了"砖，砖块"，还有"积木"的意思。如何确定一个单词确切的含义，不仅需要结合上下文的语义，还要根据常识来判断。因为此时的"我"还是个小女孩，所以我们可以推想，这里的 brick 应该是小女孩的玩具，是"积木"的意思。

4. 此处 when 引导的从句不是状语从句，而是一个非限制性定语从句，修饰先行词 time，也就是说在这段时间里，"我"几乎完全被禁止进入客厅，这段时间之所以是"dreadful time"，也正是因为大人禁止"我"进客厅玩耍。

5. 此句从字面来理解，就是被流放的人也会有和我当时同样的心情，在汉语里这样的说法似乎有点别扭，因此译者在翻译的过程中作了适当的调整，虽和原文略有不同，但作者比喻的意义没变。

6. 此句的难点在于without一词。without最常用的含义是"无,没有",因此这句话很容易被理解成客厅里没有算数、比例尺之类学习任务,而且在语义上似乎也说得通。但是结合上一句"Within…"来看作者的思路,这里用了without应该是为了和上一句形成对比(特别是将这个句子大声朗读出来的时候。顺便提一句,遇到不甚理解的句子,大声朗读出来或许是个好办法,它可以帮助我们理解),它是一个表示方位的副词,意思是"在外面"。而破折号则是为了省略前一句中已经出现的"there be"。最后,从everything来看,我们也可知道,这里的without不是介词,不是"没有"的意思,因为everything一般不用于否定的句式。

7. get in在《英汉大辞典》中的解释是"进去",但是从上下文的语境来看,那时的"我"不是能随随便便进入客厅的,因此我们推测作者可能通过一番争取才进去的,而did一词也证实了这个推测。这时,我们就需要了解get in这个动词短语的确切含义。这里,原版或双解词典可以给予我们很大的帮助。《朗文当代高级英语辞典》里,我们查到get in的释义是:to enter a place, especially when this is difficult。这证明我们的推测是正确的,因此,译者在译文中添加了"设法"二字。严谨的翻译工作者需要勤查词典,特别是查阅英文释义,即使是一个非常简单常用的单词或词语,也要通过查阅才能获悉其完整的意思。

8. 这里的came to view是英语中的习惯性表达方式,在《朗文当代高级英语词典》中可以查到,come to do something的英文释义是begin to have a feeling or opinion,因此这里的意思是"我"慢慢地开始将客厅当作剧院了。注意,这里的Theatre首字母大写,作者又生活在伦敦,由此推想应该是伦敦大剧院。那么,为什么Theatre前面还有个不定冠词a呢?我们还可以再查一查《朗文当代高级英语词典》第四版第一页a,它的第14个义项是:used before a name to mean someone or something that has the same qualities as that person or thing,那么这里的意思就不难理解了。

9. 忒修斯,希腊神话中的英雄,也是莎士比亚剧中的人物。

10. 罗伯特·布朗宁(1812—1889),英国诗人、剧作家。主要作品有《戏剧抒情诗》(*Dramatic Lyrics*),《环与书》(*The Ring and the Book*),诗剧《巴拉塞尔士》(*Paracelsus*)。

11. 这里是两个倒装句,表达作者的愿望。这一句的难点在于pictures一词,picture的意思是"图画,照片",从原文来看,这里的pictures是"我"的身影映在窗户里构成的一幅幅图画。理解这一点以后,这个句子就容易翻译了。

(译注/唐毅)

Is Love an Art?
爱是一门艺术吗？

by *Eric Fromme*

文/埃里克·弗罗姆　译/唐毅

译者按：埃里克·弗罗姆(1900—1980)，美籍德国犹太人，人本主义哲学家和精神分析心理学家。本文是他为《爱的艺术》所作的序。在大多数人看来，爱是一件很容易的事，并不需要学习。而作者的看法正好相反。他认为爱是一门艺术，要求人们有这方面的知识并付出努力。作者对产生这一错误思想的原因进行了分析，并理性地指出要掌握爱这门艺术，既要学习理论知识，又要经过大量的实践，最重要的是要将爱的艺术看得高于一切。

Is love an art? Then it requires knowledge and effort[1]. Or is love a pleasant sensation, which to experience is a matter of chance, something one "falls into" if one is lucky? This little book is based on the former premise, while undoubtedly the majority of people today believe in the latter.

Not that people think that love is not important. They are starved for it; they watch endless numbers of films about happy and unhappy love stories, they listen to hundreds of trashy songs

爱是一门艺术吗？如果爱是一门艺术，那就需要掌握有关知识并为之付出努力。抑或爱是一种愉快的感觉？能否经历看人运气，只有幸运之人，才会"坠入爱河"。这本小书是以第一种观点为前提，而今天大多数人无疑却相信后者。

人们并非认为爱不重要，相反人们极其渴望爱。或喜或悲的爱情片，人们看了不计其数，蹩脚的情歌他们百听不厌——可是几乎没有人认为

about love[2]—yet hardly anyone thinks that there is anything that needs to be learned about love.

This peculiar attitude is based on several premises which either singly or combined tend to uphold it. Most people see the problem of love primarily as that of being loved, rather than that of loving, of one's capacity to love. Hence the problem to them is how to be loved, how to be lovable. In pursuit of this aim they follow several paths. One, which is especially used by men, is to be successful, to be powerful and rich as the social margin of one's position permits. Another, used especially by women, is to make oneself attractive, by cultivating one's body, dress, etc. Other ways of making oneself attractive, used both by men and women, are to develop pleasant manners, interesting conversation, to be helpful, modest, inoffensive. Many of the ways to make oneself lovable are the same as those used to make oneself successful, "to win friends and influence people". As a matter of fact, what most people in our culture mean by being lovable is essentially a mixture[3] between being popular and having sex appeal.

A second premise behind the attitude that there is nothing to be learned about love is the assumption that the problem of love is the problem of an object, not the problem of faculty. People think that to love is simple, but that to find the right object to love—or to be loved by—is difficult. This attitude has several reasons rooted in the development of modern society. One reason is

爱是需要学习的。

这种奇怪的态度来自几种错误观念,这些观念或单独或共同地都支持这种态度。大多数人认为所谓爱就是被人爱,而非去爱别人,亦非指爱的能力。因此,对他们来说爱就是如何让自己被人所爱,如何惹人喜爱。他们通过多种途径来达到这一目的。其中一条途径尤为男性所用,就是要在其社会地位允许的范围内获得成功,获得最大的权力和最多的财富。另一条途径尤为女性所用,就是在自己的身体和衣着上下功夫,使自己变得魅力四射。另外一些方法则为男女共用,如培养得体的举止、风趣的谈吐,乐于助人,谦虚温和。许多让自己令人爱慕的方法与追求成功的途径相同,都是去"赢得朋友,影响他人"。实际上,在我们的文化中,大多数人所说的"令人爱慕",其本质是既要受人欢迎,又要能吸引异性。

导致"爱情无须学习"这种心态的第二个错误观念是认为爱的问题是"对象"问题而非"能力"问题。人们通常认为爱是很简单的事,难的是找到合适的对象——或者说爱自己的人。造成这种心态有多种原因,均根源于现代社会的发展。一是20世纪人们在恋爱对象的选择上发生了

the great change which occurred in the twentieth century with respect to the choice of a "love object". In the Victorian age, as in many traditional cultures, love was mostly not a spontaneous personal experience which then might lead to marriage. On the contrary, marriage was contracted by convention—either by the respective families, or by a marriage broker[4], or without the help of such intermediaries; it was concluded on the basis of social considerations, and love was supposed to develop once the marriage had been concluded. In the last few generations the concept of romantic love has become almost universal in the Western world. In the United States, while considerations of a conventional nature are not entirely absent, to a vast extent people are in search of "romantic love", of the personal experience of love which then should lead to marriage. This new concept of freedom in love must have greatly enhanced the importance of the object as against the importance of the function.

Closely related to this factor is another feature characteristic of contemporary culture. Our whole culture is based on the appetite for buying, on the idea of mutually favorable exchange. Modern man's happiness consists in the thrill of looking at the shop windows, and in buying all that he can afford to buy, either for cash or on installments. He(or she)[5] looks at people in a similar way. For the man an attractive girl—and for the woman an attractive man—are the prizes they are after.

很大的变化。在维多利亚时代，同许多传统文化一样，大多数情况下，爱情大多并非那种自然产生的、进而有可能发展为婚姻的个人情感体验。相反，那时的婚姻是按传统订立的契约——或由双方家庭安排，或由人从中撮合，还有的也无须中间人帮助。婚姻是在权衡了双方相关的社会因素后缔结的，而且人们认为爱情可以在结婚后培养。在过去的几个世代中，西方世界已普遍接受了浪漫爱情的概念。在美国，虽然传统的婚姻观念还没完全消失，但在很大的程度上，人们都在追求"浪漫的爱情"，追求能够走向婚姻的个人爱情体验。这种"恋爱自由"的新观念，对于爱的"对象"重于爱的"功能"的思想，一定起了很大的推动作用。

与此密切相关的是当代文化的另一特点。我们的整个文化全都建立在购买欲和互利交换的观念之上。因此现代人的幸福在于看到商店橱窗时的兴奋、在于能购买想买的东西，不管用现金还是靠分期付款。他们看人亦是如此。迷人的女子乃君子所求；迷人的男子，亦女子所求也。"迷人"通常是指在这个"人"的市场上广受欢迎、受到众人

"Attractive" usually means a nice package of qualities which are popular and sought after on the personality market. What specifically makes a person attractive depends on the fashion of the time, physically as well as mentally. During twenties, a drinking and smoking girl, tough and sexy, was attractive; today the fashion demands more domesticity and coyness. At the end of the nineteenth and the beginning of this century, a man had to be aggressive and ambitious[6]—today he was to be social and tolerant—in order to be an attractive "package". At any rate, the sense of falling in love develops usually only with regard to such human commodities as are within reach of one's own possibilities for exchange. I am out for a bargain[7]; the object should be desirable from the standpoint of its social value, and at the same time should want me, considering my overt and hidden assets and potentialities. Two persons thus fall in love when they feel they have found the best object available on the market, considering the limitations of their own exchange values. Often, as in buying real estate, the hidden potentialities which can be developed play a considerable role in this bargain. In a culture in which the marketing orientation prevails, and in which material success is the outstanding value, there is little reason to be surprised that human love relations follow the same pattern of exchange which governs the commodity and the labor market[8].

The third error leading to the assumption that

追逐的一系列特质。具体是什么特质让一个人无论是外表上还是思想上让人着迷,均取决于当时的时代潮流。二十年代,抽烟喝酒、泼辣性感的女孩是迷人的;而今天的潮流则要求女孩贤惠顾家、羞怯腼腆。在19世纪末、本世纪初,男人必须有闯劲有抱负才算是一个迷人的"综合体";而今天他们得会社交,能包容。无论如何,通常只有当对方这个商品在他的交换能力之内,一个人才会产生爱的感觉。如果我想做一笔交易,那么我的"对象"从其社会价值上来讲应该是值得要的,同时就我公开的和非公开的资产和潜力来讲,我也是对方想要的。这样,当男女双方在考虑到自身的全部交换价值后,都认为在市场上找到了最好的"对象"时,他们就坠入爱河了。这和购买不动产一样,在这笔交易中,有待开发的、还未显现的价值潜力往往起到相当大的作用。在市场化大行其道、物质成功成为首要价值的文化中,人类的爱情关系同样遵循商品市场和劳动力市场的交换模式也就不足为奇了。

导致"爱情无须学习"这种错误

there is nothing to be learned about love lies in the confusion between the initial experience of "falling" in love, and the permanent state of being in love, or as we might better say, of "standing" in love. If two people who have been strangers, as all of us are, suddenly let the wall between them break down, and feel close, feel one, this moment of oneness is one of the most exhilarating, most exciting experiences in life. It is all the more wonderful and miraculous for persons who have been shut off, isolated, without love. This miracle of sudden intimacy is often facilitated if it is combined with, or initiated by, sexual attraction and consummation. However, this type of love is by its very nature not lasting. The two persons become well acquainted, their intimacy loses more and more its miraculous character, until their antagonism, their disappointments, their mutual boredom kill whatever is left of the initial excitement. Yet, in the beginning they do not know all this: in fact, they take the intensity of the infatuation, this being "crazy" about each other, for proof of the intensity of their love, while it may only prove the degree of their preceding loneliness[9].

This attitude—that nothing is easier than to love—has continued to be the prevalent idea about love in spite of the overwhelming evidence to the contrary. There is hardly any activity, any enterprise, which is started with such tremendous hopes and expectations, and yet, which fails so regularly, as love. If this were the case with any

想法的第三个原因是将"坠入爱河"（falling in love）的初始体验和"身处爱中"（being in love 或者更确切地说 standing in love）的持久状态混为一谈。我们原本都是陌路人，假如当中有两人突然打破隔膜，相互亲近，融为一体，这个融合的瞬间便是生命中最美好、最激动人心的时刻，对于那些与世隔离、孤独无爱的人来说更是美妙和神奇。这突如其来的亲密感，如果伴以两性间的互相吸引和肉体的结合，或者由其促成，往往还会变得更加神奇。然而，这种爱情就其本质而言并不能持久。男女双方越来越了解，他们之间的亲密感也就越来越丧失其神奇性，直到有一天，相互之间的对抗、失望和厌倦将最初那点所剩无几的激情全部扼杀为止。然而，在相爱之初，他们又何曾知道这些。事实上，他们还将这如痴如醉的激情，当成了他们热烈相爱的证据，然而这只不过是证明了他们从前是多么地孤单和寂寞。

尽管有大量相左的证据，但人们却一直认为"爱是最容易不过的事情"，且这种看法经久不衰。几乎没有什么活动、没有什么事业像爱情那样，以如此巨大的希望和期许开始，又如此屡屡以失败告终。如果任何其他活动出现了这种情况，人们都会急切地

other activity, people would be eager to know the reasons for the failure, and to learn how one could do better—or they would give up the activity. Since the latter is impossible in the case of love, there seems to be only one adequate way to overcome the failure of love—to examine the reasons for this failure, and to proceed to study the meaning of love.

The first step to take is to become aware that love is an art, just as living is an art; if we want to learn how to love we must proceed in the same way we have to proceed if we want to learn any other art, say music, painting, carpentry, or the art of medicine or engineering.

What are the necessary steps in learning any art?[10]

The process of learning an art can be divided conveniently into two parts: one, the mastery of the theory; the other, the mastery of the practice. If I want to learn the art of medicine, I must first know the facts about the human body, and about various diseases. When I have all this theoretical knowledge, I am by no means competent in the art of medicine. I shall become a master in this art only after a great deal of practice, until eventually the results of my theoretical knowledge and the results of my practice are blended into one—my intuition, the essence of the mastery of any art. But, aside from learning the theory and practice, there is a third factor necessary to becoming a master in any art—the mastery of the art must be a

去了解失败的原因,去学习如何做得更好——否则干脆放弃。既然不可能放弃爱情,那么似乎也只有一个办法去克服失败了,那就是检讨失败的原因,继续探寻爱的真谛。

第一步就是要认识到,爱和生活一样,也是一门艺术。我们若想学会怎么去爱,就必须像学习其他艺术,如音乐、绘画、木工或是医学、工程一样去开展学习。

那么,学习任何一门艺术时都必须经历哪些步骤呢?

学习一门艺术的过程可简单分为两个部分:一是理论学习;二是实践。如果我想要学习医学这门艺术,首先就必须了解人体的构造,以及各种各样的疾病。但即便我掌握了全部这些理论知识,我还是不能胜任医学工作。只有经过大量实践,最终让我的理论知识和实践结合起来,将其融会贯通成为直觉,我才算是掌握了这门艺术。掌握一门艺术的实质就是是否形成直觉。但是,要成为一门艺术的大师,除了理论学习和实践以外还有第三个因素必不可少——那就是必须把精通这门艺术作为自己的终极追求,必须

matter of ultimate concern; there must be nothing else in the world more important than the art. This holds true for music, for medicine, for carpentry—and for love. And, maybe, here lies the answer to the question of why people in our culture try so rarely to learn this art, in spite of their obvious failures: in spite of the deep-seated craving for love, almost everything else is considered to be more important than love: success, prestige, money, power—almost all our energy is used for the learning of how to achieve these aims, and almost none to learn the art of loving[11].

Could it be that only those things are considered worthy of being learned with which one can earn money or prestige, and that love, which "only" profits the soul, but is profitless in the modern sense, is a luxury we have no right to spend much energy on[12]? However this may be, the following discussion will treat the art of loving in the sense of the foregoing divisions: first I shall discuss the theory of love—and this will comprise the greater part of the book; and secondly I shall discuss the practice of love—little as can be said about practice in this, as in any other field.

要将这门艺术看成高于一切。音乐、医学、木工手艺如此,爱情亦然。那么,虽然人们在爱情方面常常失败,但为何在我们的文化中很少有人去学习这门爱的艺术呢?答案或许就在这里——尽管人们心底深处都渴望爱,但他们几乎都将其他的一切,成功、名望、钱财、权力,看得比爱情重要:——我们所有的精力几乎都用来学习怎样实现这些目标,哪里还有精力学习爱的艺术呢?

难道只有那些能够带来名利的东西才值得学习吗?照现在的看法,难道"只能"滋养灵魂的爱情,是无利可图的奢侈品,我们无权耗费精力去追求吗?不管怎样,以下对爱的艺术的探讨将沿用上述分类:首先将探讨爱的理论——这将占据本书的大部分篇幅;然后将探讨爱的实践——和其他领域一样,能说的实践问题并不多。

▶ 注释:

1. 此处根据语义进行了增补,目的是使译文的意思表达更加清楚。

2. 译者将句中的两个宾语提前,以增强句子的表现力。

3. mixture 在词典里的解释是 a combination of two or more different things, feelings, or types of people,此处可以理解为多种特性的混合。但如果简单地将其译为"混合物",则显

得过于"洋腔洋调"。因此这里借用了"既要……又要……"这一句式进行翻译,使译文不仅充分传达出原文的意思,句子也显得自然地道。

4. 此句很容易让人想到"父母之命,媒妁之言"一说,似乎语义也契合,但毕竟中国文化意味太浓,还是慎用。

5. 在翻译时考虑到汉语的习惯,此处的 he(or she)译为"他们"。

6. aggressive 和 ambitious 是近义词,都表示有抱负之意,但 aggressive 更强调"活跃有为,积极进取"之意。因此译者将此处理为"有闯劲"更为准确。同时这两个形容词分别译为"有闯劲有抱负",分别从思想和行动上描述了对男性的社会要求,完全契合原文的意思。

7. 此处 be out for bargain 若理解为"出去交易"不合常理。其实 be out for something 是一个习语,词典中给出的解释是 to have a particular intention,因此这里译为"我想做一笔交易"。

8. 遇到这样复杂的长句,首先要理清句子的结构。可以看出,逗号之前,虽是一个很长的结构,但是它只是一个简单的介词短语 in a culture,其他则是两个由 which 引导的定语从句,均修饰 culture。明白这点后,句子就容易理解了。

9. 此句的难点在于 the intensity of the infatuation 和 the degree of their preceding loneliness 这两个抽象的名词词组。为了更加符合汉语的表达习惯,译者巧妙地分别将其化虚为实,化短语为分句,使句子通顺流畅。

10. 此处根据上下文的语义逻辑,添加了"那么"一词,起到了更好的承上启下的效果。

11. 原文为一个复杂的长句,译者采用变换语序和化繁为简的方法进行了处理,使译文读来有种一气呵成的感觉。

12. 原文是一个问句,但其实有"两问",因此译者在翻译的时候将其处理成两个反问句,且在第二问中,译者采取了拆分和变换语序的方法,使译文更加地道。

(译注/唐毅)

无 所 为 而 为[1]
Being Purposive without Purpose

朱光潜

译/顾韶阳

译者按：这篇文章是《读者》半月刊2017年21期的卷首语，出自朱光潜《谈美》"开场话"，有删改。原文是一封写给朋友的信，信中朱光潜先生为国内发生的各种变故感到痛心，与友人谈论何为"美"，以及如何"免俗"，全篇言辞恳切，语短意深。

我是从旧时代过来的人。我坚信情感比理智重要，要洗涤人心[2]，一定要从怡情养性[3]做起，一定要在饱食暖衣、高官厚禄[4]之外，别有较高尚、较纯洁的追求。要求人心净化，先要求人生美化。

人要有出世的精神[5]才可以做入世[6]的事业。现世是一个密集无缝的利害网[7]，一般人不能跳出这个圈套，所以转来转去，仍是被"利害"两个大字系住。在利害关系中，人们最不容易协调[8]，人人都把自己放在首位，欺诈、凌虐、劫夺种种罪孽

As a man from the old times, I'm firmly convinced that sensibility is more important than sense, and the purification of the human heart stems from the cultivation of aesthetic sensibilities. One ought to strive for something loftier and purer than mere material comforts and high social status. A purified heart depends on a beautified life.

Only with an outlook of other-worldliness can one achieve this-worldly success. The earthly world is a seamless web of interests, from which the ordinary people can hardly escape, so they remain firmly ensnared in spite of constant struggles. In the entanglement of interests, it's most unlikely for people to compromise with

都植根于此。

美感的世界纯粹是意象世界⁹,超出利害关系而独立存在。在创造或是欣赏艺术时,人都是从有利害关系的实用世界"搬家"到绝无利害关系的理想世界中去。艺术活动是"无所为而为"的。

我以为,无论是讲学问或是做事业的人,都要抱有一种"无所为而为"的精神。把自己所做的学问事业当作一件艺术品看待,只求满足理想和情趣,不斤斤计较利害得失,才可以有一番真正的成就。伟大的事业都出于宏远的眼界和豁达的胸襟。如果不讲究这两层,社会必趋于腐朽。

others, and everybody puts himself in the first place, hence the emergence of various vices, such as deception, bullying, plundering, and so on.

The aesthetic world is purely an ideal world, independent of the entanglement of interests. When creating or appreciating a work of art, people tend to "move" from the practical world with connection to interests into the ideal world free from interests. Artistic activities are "purposive without a purpose".

For my part, whoever engaged in academic study or great venture should attain to this outlook of "being purposive without purpose". True achievements cannot be made unless they view what they do as a work of art which satisfies their aspirations and tastes and care the least about interests. Success in great venture lies in wide vision and broad mind, without which the society is sure to become corrupted.

注释:

1. "无所为而为"原属儒家心性之学对孟子"义利之辨"的阐释,从老子"无为无不为"演化而来,此处意谓审美活动出自人的趣味或感性诉求,与实用目的无关,通常译为"doing for nothing"或"doing things solely for its own sake"。朱光潜在《谈美》中以"无所为而为的观赏"(disinterested contemplation)来阐释康德美学,故而"无所为而为"可以译作"doing things disinterestedly"。译者最终将其译为"being purposive without purpose",期望得到形神具备的效果。

2. "洗涤人心"指净化人的心灵,译为"the purification of the human heart"。

3. 通常情况下,"怡情养性"译为"to cultivate the inner tranquility and to nourish the soul"。但在此文中,"怡情养性"指提高审美感知力,而非传统意义上性情、性格的培养,故译为"the cultivation of aesthetic sensibilities"。

4. "饱食暖衣、高官厚禄"可直译为"ample food, warm clothing, high position and handsome salary",但这样过于冗杂。译者将其概括为生活舒适与地位显赫,意译为"material comforts and high social status"。

5. "出世"为道家思想,指抛弃社会、远离世俗,通常译为"to stand aloof from the society"。译者参考冯友兰先生英文版《中国哲学简史》中的表述,将"出世的精神"译为"an outlook of other-worldliness"。

6. "入世"指处理社会中的人际关系和人事,与上文的"出世"相对应,译为"this-worldly"。

7. "利害"通常指利害得失,一般译为"gain and loss"。但在此文中,"利害网"指错综复杂的利益关系,"利害"即利益,故译为"a web of interests"。

8. "协调"通常译为"to reconcile"或"to reach a consensus"。但根据上下文,此处"协调"指妥协,即涉及利益问题,没人愿意让步,故译为"to compromise with others"。

9. 朱光潜在《诗论》中对"意象世界"作过解释,认为"意象世界"即理想世界,故译为"an ideal world"。有人往往将其译作"an imagery world",不可取,因为此"意象"非文学中的"image"。

(译注/顾韶阳)

往事
Memories

冰 心

译/顾韶阳

译者按：这篇短小隽永的散文诗是《往事》的第三则，作者用清新淡雅的笔触，形象生动的语言描写了荷叶为红莲遮风挡雨那动人的一幕，进而引申到母亲为子女无私地奉献，表现了母爱的伟大。

父亲的朋友送给我们两缸莲花[1]，一缸是红的，一缸是白的，都摆在院子里。

八年之久，我没有在院子里看莲花了——但故乡的园院里，却有许多；不但有并蒂[2]的，还有三蒂的，四蒂的，都是红莲。

九年前的一个月夜，祖父和我在园里乘凉。祖父笑着和我说："我们园里最初开三蒂莲的时候，正好家庭中添了你们三个姊妹。大家都欢喜，说是应了花瑞[3]。"

A friend of my father's gave us two vats of lotus, one being red, the other white, both of which were put in the courtyard.

I haven't seen lotus in the courtyard for as long as eight years, but back at home in the yard there was a profusion of them: some were twin lotus flowers on one stalk, others triples, even quadruples, all of which were red.

On a moon-lit night nine years ago, my grandfather and I were relaxing in the cool yard. He said to me, smiling, "you three sisters were born at the time when the triples were in full bloom. The whole family were pleased, saying your births were a response to the flower sign of

半夜里听见繁杂的雨声[4],早起是浓阴的天,我觉得有些烦闷。从窗内往外看时,那一朵白莲已经谢了,白瓣儿小船般散漂在水面。梗上只留个小小的莲蓬[5],和几根淡黄色的花须[6]。那一朵红莲,昨夜还是菡萏的,今晨却开满了,亭亭地在绿叶中间立着。

仍是不适意![7]——徘徊了一会子,窗外雷声作了,大雨接着就来,愈下愈大[8]。那朵红莲,被那繁密的雨点,打得左右欹斜[9]。在无遮蔽的天空之下[10],我不敢下阶去,也无法可想[11]。

对屋里母亲唤着,我连忙走过去,坐在母亲旁边——回头忽然看见红莲旁边的一个大荷叶,慢慢地倾侧了来,正覆盖在红莲上面……我不宁的心绪散尽了!雨势并不减退[12],红莲却不摇动了[13]。雨点不住地打着,只能在那勇敢慈怜的荷叶上面,聚了些流转无力[14]的水珠。

我心中深深地受了感动——

母亲呵!你是荷叶,我是红莲,心中的雨点来了,除了你,谁是我在无遮拦天空下的荫蔽[15]?

auspiciousness."

The rain kept pelting down during the night, and early in the morning the sky was overcast. I felt a sense of uneasiness. Looking out of the window, I saw the white lotus flower had withered, its white petals scattering on the water like small boats. There remained on the stem a tiny seedpod, and some jasmine pistils. The red lotus, a bud last night, was in full blossom this morning, standing gracefully among the green leaves.

The sense of uneasiness was nagging at me—lingering for a while, I heard the crash of thunder, followed by a heavy rain, with ever-intensifying force. The red lotus was knocked from side to side by the pounding raindrops. I dared not go down the steps and expose myself in the heavy rain for your rescue. How powerless I was!

Mother was calling me in the opposite room, so I hurried to sit by her side—turning around, I suddenly saw a big lotus leaf leaning down and sheltering the red lotus from the rain. My uneasiness dissipated. The rain showed no sign of abating, but the red lotus could hold its stance. The incessant onslaught of the rain could only gather feeble drops on the benign, loving leaf.

I was deeply moved—

Mother! You are the lotus leaf while I am the red lotus. When it rains in my heart, who else but you could shelter me from the pouring rain?

注释：

1. 本文中"莲花"出现多次，可以区别处理。未开的莲花叫菡萏，可以译成"lotus bud"，已开的可以译成"lotus flower"或"lotus"。

2. "并蒂莲"是指并排地长在同一茎上的两朵莲花，译作"twin lotus flowers on one stalk"。三蒂莲和四蒂莲分别译作"triples""quadruples"。

3. "应了花瑞"是说花预示的好运很灵验，译为"be a response to the flower sign of auspiciousness"。

4. "繁杂的雨声"，这里的"繁杂"并非凌乱的意思，不宜译成"disorderly"；其实是指雨下得很密集，声响很大，译成"the rain kept pelting down"。下文"繁密的雨点"意思相近，译法稍有不同(pounding raindrops)。

5. 莲蓬：莲花开过后的花托，倒圆锥形，里面有莲子，译为"seedpod"。

6. 花须：花蕊，译作"pistil"。

7. "仍是不适意"，说明作者心头的烦闷、不安并未去除，译为"The sense of uneasiness was nagging at me"。

8. "愈下愈大"译成一个介词短语"with ever-intensifying force"。

9. 欹(qī)斜：歪斜不正，译作"be knocked from side to side"。

10. "无遮蔽的天空之下"未直译，而是处理为"把自己暴露在大雨下"(exposed myself in the heavy rain)。

11. "也无法可想"，译成一个感叹句，表达作者的无奈和惋惜之情。

12. "雨势并不减退"译成"the rain showed no sign of abating"，也可以译作"the rain didn't let up"。

13. "不摇动"译成"hold its stance"，是反译，正译是"didn't sway"。

14. "流转无力的"说明雨水的威力减弱了，不能再奈何红莲了，译成"feeble"。

15. "谁是我在无遮拦天空下的荫蔽"处理成"谁替我遮挡大雨"(shelter me from the pouring rain)，而将"心中的雨点来了"处理成"心里下着雨"(when it rains in my heart)，形成呼应。

(译注／顾韶阳)

寂 寞
Loneliness

梁实秋

译/顾韶阳

译者按：本文选自《雅舍遗珠》，在纷扰的社会中，人的心灵往往因为受到外界的影响而疲惫。而寂寞的心境能使人进入空灵悠逸的境界，使人的心灵得到休息。作者所处的时代令人苦闷，作者需要寂寞来调适自己。当今社会、生活节奏很快，人的身心也容易疲惫，片刻的寂寞也许是达到心灵宁静的有效途径。

寂寞是一种清福[1]。我在小小的书斋里，焚起一炉香，袅袅的一缕烟线笔直的上升，一直戳到顶棚，好像屋里的空气是绝对的静止，我的呼吸都没有搅动出一点波澜似的。我独自暗暗的望着那条烟线发怔。屋外庭院中的紫丁香树还带着不少嫣红焦黄的叶子，枯叶乱枝时时的声响可以很清晰的听到，先是一小声清脆的折断声，然后是撞击着枝干的磕碰声，最后是落到空阶上的拍打声[2]。这时节，我感到了寂寞。在这寂寞中我意识到了我自己的存

Loneliness is a form of leisurely happiness. In my tiny study, incense is being burnt in the censer, with a puff of smoke curling steadily upwards to the ceiling, as if the air in the room is so still that even my breathing could not stir it up. In solitude, I stare blankly at that puff of smoke. There stands outside in the yard a lilac tree with many reddish and yellowish leaves. I can distinctly hear the dry leaves rustling and the interlaced branches breaking off: first a sharp snap, then a knock on the trunk, and finally a pat on the empty steps. At the moment I am feeling lonely. In loneliness I am aware of my existence—brief and

在——片刻的孤立的存在。这种境界并不太易得，与环境有关，但更与心境有关。寂寥不一定要到深山大泽里去寻求，只要内心清净，随便在市廛里，陋巷里，都可以感觉到一种空灵悠逸³的境界，所谓"心远地自偏"是也。在这种境界中，我们可以在想象中翱翔，跳出尘世的渣滓，与古人游。所以我说，寂寞是一种清福。

在礼拜堂里我也有过同样的经验。在伟大庄严的教堂里，从彩画玻璃透进一股不很明亮的光线⁴，沉重的琴声好像是把人的心都洗淘⁵了一番似的，我感觉到了我自己的渺小。这渺小的感觉便是我意识到自己存在的明证。因为平常连这一点点渺小之感都不会有的！

我的朋友萧丽先生卜居在广济寺里，据他告诉我，在最近一个夜晚，月光皎洁，天空如洗，他独自踱出僧房，立在大雄宝殿前的石阶上，翘首四望，月色是那样的晶明，蓊郁的树是那样的静止，寺院是那样的肃穆，他忽然顿有所悟⁶，悟到永恒，悟到自我的渺小，悟到四大皆空的境界⁷。我相信一个人常有这样经验，他的胸襟自然豁达辽阔。

isolated. It is hard to have such an awareness, for it has something to do with atmosphere, but more importantly, with mental state. You don't need to go to the remote mountains and rivers to experience loneliness; as long as you remain inwardly tranquil, you may feel a sense of transcendence even if you stay in a market or in a back alley. As Tao Yuanming puts it, "A distant heart creates a distant retreat." In our imagination, we can go beyond the earthly existence and soar freely with the ancient poets. That's why I said loneliness is a form of leisurely happiness.

I experienced something similar in the church. In a grand and magnificent church, a flash of dim light filtered through the stained glass and the low and deep music seemed to purify the human heart. I felt small and this sense of smallness was a clear proof of my awareness of the self, because at other times, such a sense of smallness was out of the question.

My friend Mr. Xiao Li dwelt at Guangji Temple. He told me that on a night a few days ago, with the moon shining bright and the sky clear blue, he paced out of the room and stood on the steps leading to the Hall of Sakyamuni. He looked to see how crystal-clear the moon was, how still the leafy trees stood, and how imposing the temple was; he came to a sudden realization of eternity, of the smallness of the self and of indifference to worldly temptations. I believe if a man frequently experiences moments of sudden

但是寂寞的清福是不容易长久享受的。它只是一瞬间的存在[8]。世间有太多的东西不时的在提醒我们，提醒我们一件煞风景的事实：我们的两只脚是踏在地上的呀！一只苍蝇撞在玻璃窗上挣扎不出，一声"老爷太太可怜可怜我这瞎子罢"[9]，都可以使我们从寂寞中间一头栽出去，栽到苦恼烦躁的漩涡里去，至于"催租吏"一类的东西之打上门来，或是"石壕吏"之类的东西半夜捉人，其足以使人败兴生气，就更不待言了。这还是外界的感触，如果自己的内心先六根不净，随时都意马心猿，则虽处在最寂寞的境地里，他也是慌成一片忙成一团，六神无主，暴躁如雷，他永远不得享受寂寞的清福。

如此说来，所谓寂寞不即是一种唯心论，一种逃避现实的现象么？也可以说是[10]。一个高蹈隐遁的人，在从前的社会里还可以存在，而且还颇受人敬重，在现在的社会里是绝对的不可能。现在似乎只有两种类型的人了，一是在现实的泥淖中打转的人，一是偶尔也从泥淖中昂起头来喘几口气的人。寂寞便是供人喘息的几口清新空气。喘过几口气之后还得耐心地低头钻进泥淖里去。所以我对于能够昂首物外的举动并不愿再多苛责。逃避现实，如果现实真能逃避，吾瘖痖以

realization, he is sure to be broad-minded.

However, this leisurely happiness bred of loneliness is a transient state of mind and can't last long. In the world many things constantly remind us of a fact which spoils our fun: we are standing on the ground. Cases such as a fly's vain attempt to go out of the shut window and a blind man's piteous begging "Have mercy on me, sir and madam" are harsh facts that drag us out of the state of loneliness and into the whirlpool of distress and unease; let alone the breaking in of "the officials pressing for payment of tax" and the forced taking of men at midnight by "press gang at the Stone Moat Village", which annoyingly dampen one's spirits. These are external factors; if one is perturbed and unsettled in mind, even in uttermost loneliness he would be hurry-scurry, disorientated and outraged, deprived of leisurely happiness.

Therefore, isn't the so-called loneliness an attitude of idealism and a phenomenon of escapism? To some extent, yes. Hermits could only exist in ancient society in which they were held in esteem, but in modern society, they are almost extinct. Nowadays, it seems that there are two types of men: those who whirl around in the mud of reality and those who come up out of the mud to draw in breaths of air. Loneliness is the fresh air one breathes in. After a few gasps, one has to remain buried in the mud with patience. So I refrain from denouncing those acts of escapism. If it could be possible to escape reality, I would be

求¹¹之！

有遇静坐经验的人该知道，最初努力把握着自己的心，叫它什么也不想，那是多么困难的事！那是强迫自己入于寂寞的手段，所谓参禅入定¹²全属于此类。我所赞美的寂寞，稍异于是。我所谓的寂寞，是随缘偶得，无须强求¹³，一霎间的妙悟也不嫌短，失掉了也不必怅惘。但凡我有一刻寂寞时，我要好好的享受它¹⁴。

more than glad to achieve it.

Those who sit in meditation know how hard it is to concentrate their mind without distractions. This way of forcing oneself into loneliness can be attributed to Buddhist practice of meditation. The loneliness I praise is slightly different. The loneliness I mean is more chanced upon than sought after, so an instant of loneliness is long enough and there is no regret if it goes by. I would enjoy every moment of loneliness, however brief it is.

▶ 注释：

1. 清福指清闲安适的福气。此文中"清福"指随缘偶得的寂寞让人能够暂时跳出现实的泥淖，昂头喘息，这是一件令人轻松愉快的事，故译为"leisurely happiness"。

2. 该句有两个独立意群：紫丁香树带着叶子；（我）可以听到枯树乱枝的声响。为符合英语表达习惯，译者对该长句进行拆分，两个意群单独成句。第二句为中文中常见的无主句，译者增添了主语"我"，并具化了"枯树乱枝的声响"——树叶的沙沙声（the dry leaves rustling）和枯枝的折断声（the interlaced branches breaking off）。译者选用拟声词 snap, knock 和 pat 再现了枯枝折断的声响——折断声、碰撞声和拍打声。

3. "空灵悠逸的境界"较难处理。结合作者援引的陶渊明的诗句"心远地自偏"可知即使身处闹市，内心清净的人也可以摆脱尘世喧嚣，达到超然物外的境界。故译者将"空灵悠逸的境界"译为"a sense of transcendence（超然存在）"。

4. "不很明亮的光线"通常译为"less bright light"，但译者觉得不妥，故译为"subdued light"。

5. 想必去过教堂的朋友都有这种感受——在肃穆的教堂里，感受到神的伟大和自身的渺小，内心变得平和，放下杂念，心无旁骛——这就是所谓的"把人的心都洗淘了一番"。"淘洗"二字若直译为"wash/clean"不能达意，因为"淘洗"实指净化人的内心，因而译为"purify（净化）"。

6. "顿然有所悟"即"顿悟（epiphany）"，可译为"a sudden realization of"。

7. "永恒""自我的渺小"和"四大皆空的境界"是顿悟到的东西,译为"eternity","the smallness of the self"和"indifference to worldly temptations"。"四大皆空"为佛教用语,指世界上的一切都是空虚的,旨在教导人们知晓物质世界的虚幻不实,不应为世俗的欲望所累,应注重心灵的修养,寻求精神上永恒的幸福。"四大皆空"意译为"indifference to worldly temptations"。

8. "但是寂寞的清福是不容易长久享受的。它只是一瞬间的存在。"这两句之间存在因果关系:因为寂寞的清福只是一瞬间的存在,所以不能长久享受。译者合并两句,意译为"However, this leisurely happiness bred of loneliness is a transient state of mind and can't last long."。

9. "一只苍蝇撞在玻璃窗上挣扎不出,一声'老爷太太可怜可怜我这瞎子罢'"是破坏人们享受寂寞的清福的两个例子,译者增译了"cases"加以总括,符合英文表达习惯;另外,译者把这两个例子名词化为"a fly's vain attempt to go out of the shut window and a blind man's piteous begging 'Have mercy on me, sir and madam'",使译文更加简洁。

10. 此为自问自答,以示强调,引起读者注意。译者相应地处理为"Therefore, isn't the so-called loneliness an attitude of idealism and a phenomenon of escapism? To some extent, yes."。

11. 译者采用了虚拟语气,表示对"逃避现实"的一种假设。"寤寐以求"并未直译为"yearn for something day and night",事实上该成语意为"迫切地希望得到某种事物",故译为"be more than glad to achieve it"。

12. "参禅入定"是佛教徒的一种修行方法,译为"Buddhist practice of meditation"。

13. 译者将"随缘偶得,无须强求"译为"be more chanced upon than sought after"(可遇而不可求)。此外,译者增译了"so(所以)"点明该句的内在逻辑关系,符合英文逻辑性强的特点:我所谓的寂寞,是随缘偶得,无须强求,(所以)一霎间的妙悟也不嫌短,失掉了也不必怅惘。

14. "however brief it is"强调了作者十分享受寂寞,不管它多么短暂。

(译注/顾韶阳)

伤 逝[1]
Remembering the Departed Friends

台静农

译/顾韶阳

译者按:《伤逝》一文是台静农表达自己对已故知己张大千和庄慕陵的怀念与追忆之作。全篇感情基调是"淡",淡得心平气和,气度从容,文字天然去雕琢,毫无斧凿痕迹。本文基调虽淡,但并非无情。他的情主要体现在细节描写中,作者写此文时已八十五岁,但老友多年前的一句话,一个神态却依然历历在目。译者翻译时要把握好文章的基调,在细节上用功夫。

今年四月二日是大千居士[2]逝世三周年祭,虽然三年了,而昔日谶谈[3],依稀还在目前。当他最后一次入医院的前几天的下午,我去摩耶精舍[4],门者告诉我他在楼上,我就直接上了楼,他看见我,非常高兴,放下笔来,我即刻阻止他说:"不要起身[5],我看你作画。"随着我就在画案前坐下。

案上有十来幅都只画了一半,等待"加工"[6],眼前是一小幅石榴,

April 2 this year is the third anniversary of Zhang Daqian's death. Although three years have passed, I can still remember the moments of our pleasant chats. One afternoon before his last hospitalization, I went to Maya Residence to see him. The doorkeeper told me he was upstairs, so I went there and found he was painting. He was pleased to see me and put down his brush immediately. I held him back, saying, "Please remain seated. I watch you painting." Then I sat down at the painting desk.

On the desk there were a dozen paintings half done, waiting for "retouching". He was working

枝叶果实，或点或染[7]，竟费了一小时的时间才完成。第二张画什么呢？有一幅未完成的梅花，我说就是这一幅罢，我看你如何下笔，也好学呢。他笑了笑说："你的梅花好啊。"其实我学写梅，是早年的事，不过以此消磨时光而已，近些年来已不再有兴趣了。但每当他的生日，不论好坏，总画一小幅送他，这不是不自量，而是借此表达一点心意，他也欣然。最后的一次生日，画了一幅繁枝，求简不得，只有多打圈圈了。他说："这是冬心啊。"[8]他总是这样鼓励我。

话又说回来了，这天整个下午没有其他客人，他将那幅梅花完成后也就停下来了。相对谈天，直到下楼晚饭。平常吃饭，是不招待酒的，今天意外，不特要八嫂拿白兰地给我喝，并且还要八嫂调制的果子酒，他也要喝，他甚赞美那果子酒好吃，于是我同他对饮了一杯。当时显得十分高兴，作画的疲劳也没有了，不觉的话也多起来了。

回家的路上我在想，他毕竟老了，看他作画的情形，便令人伤感。犹忆一九四八年大概在春夏

right now on a small picture of pomegranate. Here adding splashes of leaves, there splotches of fruits, he spent an hour finishing it up. What was to paint next? There was an unfinished picture of sprigs of plum blossom. I asked him to work on this one, so I could learn something from him. He said with a smile, "You are good at painting sprigs of plum blossom." In fact, I learned to paint them years ago as a means of whiling away the time. Recently this interest has waned. However, on his birthday I always painted for him a small picture of plum blossom as a gift, not to show off in the presence of a master, but to express my good will. He accepted it with delight. On his last birthday, I did a painting of luxuriant foliage. Unable to prune it back, I had to add more circles. He said, "this one resembles what Jin Nong painted." He always encouraged me like that.

That afternoon there were no other guests coming, and he stopped after finishing the sprigs of plum blossom. We had a casual chat till we went downstairs for dinner. Usually there was no wine served at the dinner, but that day he wanted to make an exception. Not only did he ask his wife to offer me Brandy, but also he wanted to drink the fruit wine she made. He praised the fruit wine as delicious, so we drank a toast. He appeared cheerful and his tiredness from painting was relieved. He talked more than usual without knowing it.

On my way home, I was thinking he was old after all. It was sad enough to watch the way he painted. I recalled the day when I accompanied him to

之交,我陪他去北沟故宫博物院,博物院的同人对这位大师来临,皆大欢喜,庄慕陵兄更加高兴与忙碌[9]。而大千看画的神速,也使我吃惊,每一幅作品刚一解开,随即卷起,只一过目而已,事后我问他何以如此之快,他说这些名迹,原是熟悉的,这次来看,如同访问老友一样。当然也有在我心目中某一幅某些地方有些模糊了,再来证实一下。

晚饭后,他对故宫朋友说,每人送一幅画。当场挥洒[10],不到子夜,一气画了近二十幅,虽皆是小幅,而不暇构思,着墨成趣[11],且边运笔边说话,时又杂以诙谐,当时的豪情[12],已非今日所能想象。所幸他兴致好并不颓唐,今晚看我吃酒,他也要吃酒,犹是少年人的心情,没想到这样不同寻常的兴致,竟是我们最后一次的晚餐。数日后,我去医院,仅能在加护病房见了一面,虽然一息尚存,相对已成隔世[13],生命便是这样的无情。

摩耶精舍与庄慕陵兄的洞天

Beigou Palace Museum at Beigou in late spring or early summer of 1948. The staff in the Museum gave him a hearty welcome, especially Mr. Zhuang Muling who bustled around with greater zest. I marveled at the speed with which Daqian saw a painting. No sooner had he unrolled a scroll than he rolled it up—with a fleeting glance the painting was taken in. Later I asked how he could do so, and he replied that since these famous paintings had been familiar to him, seeing them again was like meeting old friends; of course, certain parts of a particular painting might be vague in his memory, so re-seeing could help clarify them.

After dinner, he told those present in the Museum he would give each an improvised painting. He started right away, and before midnight he had finished nearly 20 works at one go. Though small in size and done without enough time for composition, these works displayed his effortless artistry. What's more, in the process of painting, he kept talking to us with witty humor. Such exuberant spirit can only remain in memory. Luckily he was not feeling dejected, instead he was envious of my drinking wine tonight and asked for a cup, as if he was as lively as a young man. Who would have thought such a dinner full of exceptional zeal could be the last one we had together. A few days later, I could only see him in the ICU of the hospital. Though lingering on with his last breath, he seemed to be retreating into another world. Such was the ruthlessness of life.

Maya Residence and Zhuang Muling's Heavenly

山堂，相距不过一华里，若没有小山坡及树木遮掩，两家的屋顶都可以看见的。慕陵初闻大千要卜居于外双溪，异常高兴，多年友好，难得结邻，如陶公与素心友"乐与数晨夕"¹⁴，也是晚年快事。大千住进了摩耶精舍，慕陵送给大千一尊大石，不是案头清供，而是放在庭园里的，好像是"反经石"之类，重有两百来斤呢。

可悲的，他们两人相聚时间并不多，因为慕陵精神开始衰惫¹⁵，终至一病不起。他们最后的相晤，还是在荣民医院里，大千原是常出入于医院的，慕陵却一去不返了。

我去外双溪时，若是先到慕陵家，那一定在摩耶精舍晚饭。若是由摩耶精舍到洞天山堂，慕陵一定要我留下同他吃酒。其实酒甚不利他的病体，而且他也不能饮了，可是饭桌前还得放一杯掺了白开水的酒，他这杯淡酒，也不是为了我，却因结习难除，表示一点酒人的倔强，听他家人说，日常吃饭就是这样的。

后来病情加重，已不能起床，我到楼上卧房看他时，他还要若

Hall were no more than 500 meters apart. The roofs of both houses could have been seen if the view had not been blocked by the hillsides and trees. Muling felt extremely happy when he heard Daqian would settle in the Outer Double Creeks. To have this old friend living next door was a real pleasure in his remaining years, just as Tao Yuanming and his simple-hearted friends "gladly got together from morning to night". After Daqian moved to Maya Residence, Muling gave Daqian a huge stone, the one not put on the desk, but laid in the yard, the so-called "the stone reversing the compass", weighing 100 kilograms.

Sadly enough, they didn't have enough time to see each other, because Muling's vitality was declining until finally he fell ill and was completely bedridden. They met each other for the last time in Veterans General Hospital. Daqian was in and out of hospital regularly, but Muling went there without return.

When I went to Outer Double Creeks, I would always dine at Maya Residence after staying for a while at Muling's. If I reached the Heavenly Hall after dropping by to Maya Residence, Muling would always detain me to drink wine with him. In fact, wine was harmful to his ill health, and he couldn't drink any more. However, he would always put in front of him a cup of wine blended with water. This cup of light wine was not served for me, but for himself as a sign of his clinging on to old habits of drinking wine. His family said he always did so at dinnertime.

Later as his illness worsened, he could no longer leave his sickbed. When I went upstairs to see him,

侠夫人下楼拿杯酒来,有时若侠夫人不在,他要我下楼自己找酒。我们平常都没有饭前酒的习惯,而慕陵要我这样的,或许以为他既没有精神谈话,让我一人枯坐着,不如喝杯酒。当我一杯在手,对着卧榻上的老友,分明死生之间,却也没生命奄忽之感[16]。或者人当无可奈何之时,感情会一时麻木的。

he asked his wife to fetch a cup of wine downstairs. Sometimes if his wife was out, he urged me to look for wine downstairs. Usually we didn't have a habit of drinking wine before dinner, and the reason why he asked me to do so was that he probably thought he was too feeble to talk, so it was better for me to drink wine than to sit idle. Holding a cup of wine, and facing the bedridden friend, I felt as if he was retreating farther away from this world, yet I didn't have a sense of how life was impermanent. Perhaps when a person was helplessly facing death, he could be emotionally insensitive for a while.

▶ 注释:

1. "伤逝"一词虽是表达作者对故友逝世的感伤,但时隔三年,译为"mourn for/grieve over the Deceased/Dead"已不甚合适且未点名"好友",此处更多的则是表达对故人的怀念,用"remember"更为合理,故而译为"Remembering the Departed Friends"。

2. 此处"大千居士"并非强调张大千是"不出家的佛教徒"或"隐居不做官的人",只不过是一种称呼,不宜译为"lay Buddhist"或"hermit",译者认为此处"居士"一词不译也无妨。

3. "譙谈"此处指"相聚叙谈",故而译为"our pleasant chats"。

4. "摩耶精舍"与后文的"洞天山堂"均为住所,译为 Maya Residence 和 Heavenly Hall。

5. 若直译为"Don't get up"或"Don't bother"都太过直白,不如采取反译法,译为"Please remain seated"。

6. "加工"此处指"润色、修饰",译为"retouch"或者"polish"。

7. "枝叶果实,或点或染"不大容易翻译,难就难在"点""染"是中国画的作法,英语中并无现成对应词。译者将"点""染"处理成名词,结合前文"枝叶果实",构成短语"splashes of leaves"和"splotches of fruits",同时增添动词"add",将整句译为"Here adding splashes of leaves, there splotches of fruits."。

8. "冬心"此处指清代书画家金农(扬州八怪之首,号冬心先生),因此译为"This one resembles what Jin Nong painted."。

9. "更加高兴与忙碌"若译为 more cheerful and busy,则显得平淡,不如译为"bustled around with greater zest",表现力更足。

10. 不能直译为 began to draw at once,此处应当强调"即兴创作"以显大千绘画艺术高超,故而译为"would give each an improvised painting"。

11. "着墨成趣"指大千作画艺术已臻化境,一落笔便意境顿出,趣味顿生,故而译为"effortless artistry"。

12. "豪情"此处并非指"豪情壮志"(lofty sentiment),而是大千先生作画时"精力充沛与热情洋溢",故而译为"exuberant spirit"。

13. "虽一息尚存,但相对已成隔世"强调作者的内心感受(即为生命的无情感到黯然神伤),"一息尚存"处理为"弥留之际(lingering on with his last breath)"。"隔世"原义指相隔一世,多形容人事、自然或社会变化巨大,比如"久别重逢,恍如隔世"。但此处"隔世"指阴阳两隔,大千虽一息尚存,但正渐行渐远去往另一个世界,故而译为"he seemed to be retreating into another world"。

14. 诗句出自陶渊明《移居二首》中的"闻多素心人,乐与数晨夕"。"素心友"即"simple-hearted friends","乐与数晨夕"译为"gladly got together from morning to night"。

15. "精神开始衰惫"即"活力不再,更显颓唐",译为"declining in vitality"。

16. "死生之间"和前文"已成隔世"类似,故译为"retreating farther away from this world","奄忽"一词旨在感叹"生命的短促无常",译为"have a sense of how life was impermanent"。

(译注/顾韶阳)

钱锺书序两则
Two Prefaces by Qian Zhongshu

译者按：序言一中，作者将"人生"比作一部大书，而这些文章是写在人生边上的随感，悠闲阅读，随手批注。序言二中，作者则警告读者不必自作多情，对号入座。

《写在人生边上》[1] 序
Preface to *Writing at the Margin of Life*

人生据说是一部大书。

假使人生真是这样，那末，我们一大半作者[2]只能算是书评家，具有书评家的本领，无须看得几页书，议论早已发了一大堆，书评一篇写完交卷[3]。

但是，世界上还有一种人。他们觉得看书的目的，并不是为了写书评或介绍。他们有一种业余消遣者的随便和从容，他们不慌不忙地浏览。每到有什么意见，他们随手[4]在书边的空白上注几个字，写一个问号或感叹号，像中国旧书上的眉批，外国书里的 marginalia。这种零星随感[5]并非他们对于整部书的结论。因为是随时批

Life is said to be one huge book.

If that's indeed the case, most of us authors are nothing more than book critics. Possessing the ability of a critic, we have made a pile of commentaries after leafing through a few pages and finished it off with a book review.

However, there is a different type of people who think the purpose of reading is not to write a book review or an introduction. They browse the book as leisurely as a casual and carefree amateur. When an opinion occurs to them, they jot down in passing a few notes or write a question mark or an exclamation mark at the margin of the book, like " headnotes " in ancient Chinese books or marginalia in foreign books. These piecemeal

识,先后也许彼此矛盾,说话过火⁶。他们也懒得去理会⁷,反正是消遣,不像书评家负有指导读者、教训作者的重大使命。谁有能力和耐心做那些事呢?

假使人生是一部大书,那末,下面的几篇散文只能算是写在人生边上的。这本书真大!一时不易看完,就是写过的边上也还留下好多空白。

一九三九年二月十八日

random thoughts are not their final judgement of the book, and as they are casually jotted down, they may contradict one another or seem overdone. The authors just leave them as they are. After all, they are just amateurs who do it for pleasure, unlike those critics who shoulder heavy responsibilities of guiding the readers and criticizing the authors. How could they have the ability and patience for such things?

If life is one huge book, the essays that follow are merely written at the margin of life. What a huge book! It's hard to read it over all at once, and the margins in which my random thoughts are jotted down are left with plenty of blank space.

February 18, 1939

《人兽鬼》序
Preface to *Humans, Beasts and Ghosts*

假使这部稿子没有遗失或烧毁,这本书有一天能够出版,序是免不了的。

节省人工的方法愈来愈进步,往往有人甘心承认⁸是小说或剧本中角色的原身,借以不费事地自登广告⁹。为防免这种冒名顶替,我特此照例声明,书里的人物情事都是凭空臆造的。不但人是安分守法的良民,兽是驯服的家畜,而且鬼也并非

If this manuscript is preserved, without being lost or burned, and one day finds its way into the press, a preface cannot be done without.

With the advance of labour-saving techniques, people tend to readily identify themselves as the models for the characters in a novel or a play so as to advertise their presence in an effortless way. To guard against this act of imposture, I declare clearly, as I always do, that the characters and events in this book are fictitious. Not only are the

没管束的野鬼；他们都只在本书范围里生活，决不越轨溜出书外。假如谁要顶认自己是这本集子里的人、兽或鬼，这等于说我幻想虚构的书中角色，竟会走出书，别具血肉、心灵和生命[10]，变成了他，在现实里自由活动。从黄土抟人[11]以来，怕没有这样创造的奇迹。我不敢梦想我的艺术会那么成功，惟有事先否认，并且敬谢[12]他抬举我的好意[13]。

三十三年(一九四四)四月一日

humans law-abiding citizens, but the beasts are tame domesticated animals, even the ghosts are not those specters who wander about unrestrained. They will never go beyond the confines of the pages. If someone should equate himself with one of the humans, beasts or ghosts in this collection, it would be tantamount to saying that a fictitious character in my book could walk out of the pages as a real person bearing his resemblance, with blood and flesh, soul and vitality, and move about freely in the real world. I'm afraid such miracle of creation is nowhere to see since man was created out of clay. I dare not dream of such artistic attainments, so I have to decline politely in advance this undeserved flattery.

April 1, 1944

◆ 注释：

1. 如果人生是一本大书，"边上"则是"页边空白"，故而译为"margin"。

2. "我们一大半作者"译为"most of us authors"，将作者自己也囊括在内，更显谦虚和严谨。

3. "写完交卷"中"交卷"可以略去不译，直接译成"finish it off"便可，表明书评家写完书评、万事大吉的态度。

4. "随手"，即"随手批注"，译为"jot down in passing a few notes"。

5. "零星随感"，理解为"零碎的，随意的感想"，译为"piecemeal random thoughts"。

6. 此处的"说话过火"即"不恰当的批注"，译为"seem overdone"即可。

7. "懒得去理会"直译为"would not bother to care"显得太过直白，不如反译为"leave them where they are"。

8. 此处"承认"不宜译为admit(承认、供认所犯的过错)，译为identify(自认为)较为合适。

9. "不费事自登广告"指借别人的书来为自己宣传,译为"to advertise their presence in an effortless way"。

10. 此处的"生命"若译为"life"则不够贴切,不妨译为"vitality",以体现这些"虚构角色"的生命力和活力。

11. 实指"女娲造人",但是本文并非重在传播中国文化,且国外也有上帝造人的传说,因此不必采取异化译法,译为"since man was created out of clay"即可。

12. "敬谢"即"礼貌地拒绝",可译为"decline politely"。

13. "抬举我的好意"暗含作者的讽刺,故而译为"undeserved flattery"。

(译注/顾韶阳)

窗 帘
Window Curtains

杨 绛

译/顾韶阳

译者按："窗帘"是杨绛先生的一篇精致小品，"窗帘"在文中具有象征意义。文章探讨的是人际间应有必要的善意的掩饰，应适当保持空间距离或心理距离，因为距离、含蓄产生美感，尊重、保留构成和谐。

人不怕挤。尽管摩肩接踵，大家也挤不到一处[1]。像壳里的仁，各自各。像太阳光里飞舞的轻尘，各自各。凭你多热闹的地方，窗对着窗，各自人家，彼此不相干。只要挂上一个窗帘，只要拉过那薄薄的一层，便把别人家隔离在千万里以外了[2]。

隔离，不是断绝[3]。窗帘并不堵没窗户，只在彼此间增加些距离——欺哄人招引人的距离。窗帘并不盖没窗户，只隐约遮掩——多么引诱挑逗的遮掩！所以，赤裸裸的窗口不引人注意，而一角掀动的窗帘，惹人窥探猜

People don't care about crowding; though shoulder rubbing shoulder, they stay apart, just like kernels in a shell taking up their respective spaces, or clouds of dust in the sun dancing in their respective ways. However bustling a place is, the households with windows facing each other remain separate. A thin curtain, if pulled closed, is capable of keeping others miles apart.

Keeping others apart doesn't mean cutting them off. A curtain doesn't block up the window; it merely increases the distance between each other—a deceiving and tempting distance. A curtain doesn't cover up the window; it merely obscures the view—what a provoking and

测,生出无限兴趣。

　　赤裸裸,可以表示天真朴素。不过,如把天真朴素做了窗帘的质料,做了窗帘的颜色,一个洁白素净的帘子,堆叠着透明的软纱,在风里飘曳,这种朴素,只怕比五颜六色[4]更富有魅力,认真要赤裸裸不加遮饰,除非有希腊神像那样完美的身体,有天使般纯洁的灵魂。培根(Bacon)说过:"赤裸裸是不体面的;不论是赤露的身体,或赤露的心。"(Nakedness is uncomely, as well in mind as body.)人从乐园里驱逐出来的时候[5],已经体味到这句话了。

　　所以赤裸裸的真实总需要些掩饰。白昼的阳光[6],无情地照彻了人间万物,不能留下些幽暗让人迷惑,让人梦想,让人希望[7]。如果没有轻云薄雾把日光筛漏出五色霞彩来,天空该多么单调枯燥!

　　隐约模糊中[8],才容许你做梦和想象。距离增添了神秘。看不见边际,变为没边没际的遥远与辽阔[9]。云雾中的山水,暗夜的星辰,希望中的未来,高超的理想,仰慕的名人,心许的"相知"[10],——隔着窗帘[11],惝怳迷离,可以产生无限美妙的想

tantalizing obscureness! Therefore, a "naked" window doesn't draw attention, whereas a curtain with a flapping corner invites an urge to peep and speculate out of immense curiosity.

Nakedness may signify innocence and simplicity. However, if innocence and simplicity are used as the texture and color of a curtain, the curtain will be quietly colored with its diaphanous gauze. Such a plain curtain fluttering in the breeze is more tantalizing than that with a riot of color. Stark nakedness is inadvisable unless you have the perfect bodies of the Greek gods and the pure souls of the angels. Francis Bacon once said, "Nakedness is uncomely, as well in mind as body." When expelled from the Garden of Eden, men understood the meaning of these words.

Therefore naked truth should more or less be concealed. The dazzling sunlight, relentlessly shining upon myriad things on earth, leaves no shadow that arouses perplexity, dream and hope. How monotonously dull the sky would be if there were no light clouds and thin mists through which the sunlight filters and turns into a rainbow of colors!

Blurred dimness leaves room for reveries and fantasies. Distance adds to the sense of mystery. A vista obscured may extend as far and wide as our endless imagination can reach. Hills and rivers veiled in mist, stars on a dark night, the future in our hopes, a lofty ideal, celebrities held in esteem, a "soulmate" of one's heart—if blurred,

象。如果你嫌恶窗帘的间隔,冒冒失失闯进门、闯到窗帘后面去看个究竟,赤裸裸的真实只怕并不经看[12]。像丁尼生(Tennyson)诗里的"夏洛特女郎"(The Lady of Shalott),看厌了镜中反映的世界,三步跑到窗前,望一望真实世界。她的镜子立即破裂成两半,她毁灭了以前快乐而无知的自己。

　　人家挂着窗帘呢,别去窥望。宁可自己也挂上一个,华丽的也好,朴素的也好。如果你不屑挂,或懒得挂[13],不妨就敞着个赤裸裸的窗口。不过,你总得尊重别人家的窗帘。

四十年代

so to speak, by a "curtain" and lost in vagueness, may arouse enchanting fantasies. If you hate the barrier of the curtain and break rashly in to take a look at what's behind, you'll probably be disillusioned by the naked truth. The Lady of Shalott in Tennyson's poem is fed up with the world in the mirror, and she rushes to the window to see the real world. The mirror cracks from side to side and her happy and innocent self is ruined.

　　There's a curtain on the window, so please don't peep inside. You'd better hang a curtain yourself, be it colorful or plain. If you disdain to do so, or if you don't feel like doing so, leave your windows "naked". However, you have to respect other people's window curtains.

1940s

▶ 注释:

1. "挤不到一处",如果直译为"don't crowd/squeeze into each other",显然不妥。译者采取了反译法,译为"stay apart"。孰优孰劣,读者自会判断。

2. "便把别人家隔离在千万里以外了",同样采取反译法,译为"is capable of keeping others miles apart"。

3. "隔离,不是断绝",有人译为"Barriers are not disconnection",直译痕迹太过,令读者困惑。译者认为,"隔离"可以沿用上文"keeping others apart",断绝可以用词组"cut off"来表示,因此译为"keeping others apart doesn't mean cutting them off"。

4. "五颜六色",译为"a riot of color",比单纯译成"colorful"更形象生动。

5. "人从乐园里驱逐出来的时候",这里是指亚当夏娃被赶出伊甸园的圣经典故,译为"When expelled from the Garden of Eden, men..."

6. "白昼的阳光","白昼"未直译为"daylight",作者只是想强调阳光刺眼,因此译为"the dazzling sunlight"。

7. "让人迷惑,让人梦想,让人希望",译为"arouses perplexity, dream and hope",简洁而又达意。

8. "隐约模糊中",译成转移修饰词"in blurred dimness",比"in dimness and obscurity"更凝练。

9. "看不见边际,变为没边没际的遥远与辽阔",这是本文揭示主题的句子,也是最难翻译的一句。有人未正确理解原文,全都采取直译法,译文晦涩难懂,可想而知。其实,这里作者想表达的是被遮掩的景色让人浮想联翩,在无穷的想象中,这些景色遥远又辽阔。翻译时译者增添主语"vista","看不见边际"用"blurred"(遮蔽的)一词对应,谓语动词的选择很关键,译者没有直译原文动词,重新选了一个动词"extend",动态感更强。同时,译者增添了"imagination"一词,想表达"只要发挥想象,前方的景色无比遥远和辽阔"。整句译为"A vista obscured may extend as far and wide as our endless imagination can reach."。

10. "心许的'相知'",这里意思相当于"心中的灵魂伴侣",译为"a 'soulmate' of one's heart"。

11. "隔着窗帘",这里"窗帘"具有象征意义,故而增添"so to speak",同时"curtain"加引号。

12. "并不经看",这里表示窗帘后的真实可能会给人带来失落感,译为"probably be disillusioned by the naked truth"。

13. "懒得挂",这里的"懒"不宜译为"lazy",译为"don't feel like doing so"。

(译注/顾韶阳)

爱
Love

张爱玲

译/顾韶阳

译者按：本文选自张爱玲的散文集《流言》(上海五洲书报社 1944 年出版)。张爱玲因其精巧、细腻的小说而蜚声海内外。这篇散文却大不相同，全文仅三百余字，语言朴素洗练、哀而不伤，借女孩子的一生，道尽了人生的酸楚与沧桑、"爱"的凄美与无望，却似又不止于此。文章于结尾处升华，为人世间的苍凉添上了一声"有缘无分"的叹息："噢，原来你也在这里吗？"

这是真的[1]。

有个村庄的小康之家的女孩子，生得美，有许多人来做媒，但都没有说成[2]。那年她不过十五六岁吧，是春天的晚上，她立在后门口，手扶着桃树。她记得她穿的是一件月白的衫子[3]。对门住的年轻人，同她见过面，可是从来没有打过招呼的，他走了过来，离得不远，站定了，轻轻地说了一声："噢，你也在这里吗？"[4] 她没有说什么，他也没有再说什么，站了一会儿，各自走开了。

It was a true story.

There was a girl from a well-off family in a village. She was pretty, and many a matchmaker was sent to seek matrimonial relations, but none of the attempts were fruitful. That year she was only fifteen or sixteen. One spring night, she was standing at the back door, her hand resting on a peach tree. She could remember she was wearing a pale blue blouse. The young man in the opposite house met her before, but they didn't greet each other. He was coming toward her, then paused at a distance and said in a soft voice, "Oh, you are

就这样就完了⁵。

后来这女子被亲眷拐了,卖到他乡外县去作妾,又几次三番地被转卖,经过无数的惊险的风波⁶,老了的时候她还记得从前那一回事,常常谈起,在那春天的晚上,在后门口的桃树下,那年轻人⁷。

于千人万人之中遇见你所要遇见的人,于千万年之中,时间的无涯的荒野里⁸,没有早一步,也没有晚一步,刚巧赶上了,那也没有别的话可说,惟有轻轻的问一声:"噢,你也在这里吗?"

also here." She didn't say anything, and he didn't say anything more either. Standing for a while, they went their separate ways.

That was how the story ended.

Later on the girl was abducted by her relative and sold far away to a man as his concubine. She was resold several times and suffered untold terrible misfortunes. When she was old she could still remember, and kept talking about, that spring night when she stood under the peach tree at the back door, meeting the young man.

When you meet, among thousands of people, the very person you're meant to meet and when you chance upon him/her at the very moment, neither too early nor too late, in the endless flow of desolate existence, you can say nothing except murmuring a greeting, "Oh, you are also here."

注释:

1. "这是真的。"首段仅四字,分量却极重。开篇即强调本文所叙是真的故事,并非小说或传奇,故译为 It was a true story。这句话奠定了全文的感情基调,文章无一华丽辞藻,却笼罩着一层淡淡的轻愁,于无声处揭开隐秘的伤痛。

2. "做媒"译为 seek matrimonial relations,"媒人"为 matchmaker,"没有说成"意指"做媒的尝试未果",译为 none of the attempts were fruitful。

3. "月白"为"淡蓝色",故译为 pale blue。女孩子穿的"衫子"应为 blouse。

4. "噢,你也在这里吗?"译为"Oh, you are also here.",这句对白看似寻常,却是文眼所在。原文意不在发问,也不求回答,表达的是邂逅的惊喜,故译为陈述句。

5. "就这样就完了。"译为"That was how the story ended.",与前文的"It was a true story."相呼应。就是这样简单的故事,尚未开始就不得不结束,更加重了文章的悲剧性。

6. "风波"在此处指"不幸、灾难",译为 misfortunes。

7. "从前那一回事"译者略去不译,同时将"记得"和"常常谈起"并列,宾语为"春天的晚上","站在后门口的桃树下"为时间状语,将"那年轻人"置于句尾,增添"meeting"一词,构成现在分词短语。这样,译者试图将时间、空间、人物串联起来,同时突出人物,表达有缘无分的无奈和怅惘之情。

8. "时间的无涯的荒野里"较难处理,如果直译成"in the wildness of endless time",未尝不可,但总觉得意犹未尽。译者最后处理为"in the endless flow of desolate existence",其中"flow"一词旨在表达"岁月之流淌","existence"表达"生命的存在",而"desolate"是译者精心挑选的一语双关之词,既指"凄凉",又暗含"孤独"。

(译注/顾韶阳)

成 功
Success

季羡林

译/顾韶阳

译者按:这篇散文收录在季羡林先生的散文精选《季羡林谈人生》中。话题虽然是老生常谈,但是凝聚了作者的毕生治学经验,见解独到,引经据典,具有很强的说服力和感染力。

什么叫成功?顺手拿过[1]一本《现代汉语词典》,上面写道:"成功,获得预期的结果。"言简意赅,明白之至。

但是,谈到"预期",则错综复杂,纷纭混乱。人人每时每刻每日每月[2]都有大小不同的预期,有的成功,有的失败,总之是无法界定,也无法分类,我们不去谈它。

我在这里只谈成功,特别是成功之道。这又是一个极大的题目,我却只是小做[3]。积七八十年之经验,我得到下面这个公式:天资+勤奋+机遇=成功。

What is success? According to *The Contemporary Chinese Dictionary*, success is defined as "achieving the desired or hoped-for results". The definition is concise and easy to understand.

However, the word "desired" causes confusion due to its complexity. At any moment each of us cherishes desires in various degrees: some fulfilled, others unfulfilled. Anyway, they defy our definition and classification, so we'd better leave them untouched.

Let's keep to success, especially the way of success. That's a very big topic, and I'll make little of it. In accordance with my experience of the past seventy to eighty years, I work out the following equation: Talent + diligence + opportunity = success.

120

"天资",我本来想用"天才",但天才是个稀见现象,其中不少是"偏才"⁴,所以我弃而不用,改用"天资",大家一看就明白。这个公式实在过分简单化了,但其中的含义是清楚的。搞得太繁琐,反而不容易说清楚。

谈到天资,首先必须承认,人与人之间天资是不同的,这是一个事实,谁也否定不掉。十年浩劫中,自命天才的人居然号召大批天才⁵。葫芦里卖的是什么药,至今不解。到了今天,学术界和文艺界自命天才的人颇不稀见,我除了羡慕这些人"自我感觉过分良好"外,不敢赞一词⁶。对于自己的天资,我看,还是客观一点好,实事求是一点好。

至于勤奋,一向为古人所赞扬。囊萤映雪、悬梁刺股等故事⁷流传了千百年,家喻户晓。韩文公的"焚膏油以继晷,恒兀兀以穷年"⁸,更为读书人所向往。如果不勤奋,则天资再高也毫无用处。事理至明,无待饶舌。

I had intended to use "genius" instead of "talent", but geniuses are rare and many of them are so-called "one-trick ponies", hence my present choice is "talent", a word that may avoid ambiguity for the reader. The equation is too simplified, but what it signifies is clear. Undue complication may add to the difficulty of explaining it clearly.

In terms of "talent", it should be acknowledged as an undeniable fact that people differ from one another in their talent. During the Decade of Turmoil, those who considered themselves geniuses called on us to denounce geniuses, and even today I am not clear what nasty tricks they had up their sleeve. Nowadays in the academic, literary and artistic circles, there are plenty of people who consider themselves geniuses, their "undue self-complacency" is really enviable, but I grudge offering them a word of comment. As I see it, it is advisable to take an objective, a down-to-earth attitude toward one's talent.

As for "diligence", it has long been a virtue lavishly lauded by the ancients. Stories such as "reading by the light of bagged fireflies or the reflected light of snow" or "tying one's hair on the beam and jabbing one's side with an awl to keep oneself awake during reading" have been passed down from generation to generation and are known to everyone. Han Yu's famous lines "burning oil to stretch the sun's shadow, working assiduously all year round" have long been an inspiring example for scholars to follow. Talent, however great it is, is of no use if unsupported by

谈到机遇，往往被人所忽视。它其实是存在的，而且有时候影响极大。就以我为例，如果清华不派我到德国去留学，则我的一生完全不会像现在这个样子。

把成功的三个条件拿来分析一下，天资是由"天"来决定的，我们无能为力。机遇是不期而来的，我们也无能为力。只有勤奋一项是我们自己决定的，我们必须在这一项上狠下功夫。在这里，古人的教导也多得很。还是先举韩文公。他说："业精于勤，荒于嬉；行成于思，毁于随[9]。"这两句话是大家都熟悉的。

王静安在《人间词话》[10]中说，"古今之成大事业、大学问者，必须经过三种之境界[11]：'昨夜西风凋碧树，独上高楼，望尽天涯路[12]。'此第一境也。'衣带渐宽终不悔，为伊消得人憔悴[13]。'此第二境也。'众里寻他千百度，回头蓦见，那人正在，灯火阑珊处[14]。'此第三境也"。静安先生第一境写的是预期。第二境写的是勤奋。第二境写的是成功。其中没有写天资和机遇。我不敢说，这

diligence. This is a self-evident truth which needs no further explanation.

"Opportunity" as a factor is often overlooked; it actually exists and is sometimes of vital importance. Take myself as an example: if Tsinghua University had not sent me to Germany for advanced study, my life would have been totally different from what it is today.

By analyzing the three factors responsible for success, we know that "talent" is predestined by "fate" and we can do little about it. We also know that "opportunity" comes by chance and again we can do little about it. "Diligence" is the only factor in which we have a say, so we have to put in utmost effort in order to succeed. Teachings about this are abundant in ancient books. Again let's quote two well-known sentences by Han Yu, "The progress of learning is made through diligence and checked by idleness. Achievements arise from independent thinking rather than blind imitation."

Wang Guowei said in *Annotations and Comments on Poems*: "Throughout the ages, all those who have been highly successful in great ventures and in the pursuit of learning must have gone through three stages. 'Last night the west wind withered the green trees. Alone I climb up the high tower to look as far as the road reaches the distant horizon.' That is the first stage. 'I never regret getting thinner with my clothes being looser than ever. For you I am thus pining away in deep yearning.' That is the second stage. 'I have been seeking her in the crowd for numerous times. All of a sudden I turn around, only to find her where the

是他的疏漏,因为写的角度不同。但是,我认为,补上天资与机遇,似更为全面。我希望,大家都能拿出"衣带渐宽终不悔"的精神来从事做学问或干事业,这是成功的必由之路。

lamplight is fading. ' That is the third stage. " What Mr. Wang Guowei illustrated as the first stage is desired results, the second stage diligence and the third stage success. He didn't mention talent and opportunity. This, of course, is not a matter of carelessness, but a matter of perspective from which he approached the subject. However, I would say his view would have been made complete if talent and opportunity had been added. I hope everyone engaged in academic study or great venture can do his uttermost and "never regret getting thinner with his clothes being looser than ever". This is the only path leading to success.

注释:

1. "顺手拿过",有的人会译为"at hand"或是"handy",但译者认为这里不译也无妨。

2. "每时每刻每日每月",此处不能字字死译,应该灵活变通,译为"at any moment"。

3. "小做",意思是"从小处着手",译为"make a little of"。

4. "偏才"这里是说"在某方面有特殊才能的人",可译作"specially talented in certain areas/fields",但英语中有类似的表达,"one-trick ponies"。

5. "大批天才",这里是指"文革"时期兴起的大肆批判的现象,此处的"批"是"批判、批斗"的意思,因此译为"denounce geniuses"。

6. "不敢赞一词",即"不赞一词",意思是无话可说,因此译为"grudge offering them a word of comment"。

7. "囊萤映雪、悬梁刺股等故事",这里的"囊萤映雪"和"悬梁刺股"都是中国古代的成语故事,译者作为中国文化的传播者,译文中应涵盖故事中所有的意象,因此译为"Stories such as "reading by the light of bagged fireflies or the reflected light of snow" or "tying one's hair on the beam and jabbing one's side with an awl to keep oneself awake during reading""。

8. "焚膏油以继晷,恒兀兀以穷年",这句话出自唐代韩愈的《进学解》,意思是"太阳下去了,就燃起油灯,一年到头,永远在那里孜孜不倦地研究。形容夜以继日地用功读书,全年都勤奋不懈",此处译为"burning oil to stretch the sun's shadow, working assiduously all year

round"。

9. "业精于勤,荒于嬉;行成于思,毁于随",这句话也是出自唐代韩愈的《进学解》。意思是"学业由于勤奋而精通,但它却能荒废在游戏玩耍中。事情由于反复思考而成功,但它却能毁灭于不经大脑的随性中"。此处译为"The progress of learning is made through diligence and checked by idleness. Achievements arise from independent thinking rather than blind imitation."。

10. 《人间词话》是王国维所著的一部文学批评著作,意译为 Annotations and Comments on Poems。

11. "境界",此处不能译为"realm",用词要能体现出不同境界的层次感,因此译为"stage"。

12. "昨夜西风凋碧树,独上高楼,望尽天涯路",这句话出自北宋晏殊的《蝶恋花·槛菊愁烟兰泣露》,意为"昨夜西风惨烈,凋零了绿树。我独上高楼,望尽那消失在天涯的道路。"该句重点在于对"望尽天涯路"的翻译,译者用"reach"一词来体现"望尽"之意境。全句译为"Last night the west wind withered the green trees. Alone I climb up the high tower to look as far as the road reaches the distant horizon."。

13. "衣带渐宽终不悔,为伊消得人憔悴",这句话出自宋代词人柳永所作的《蝶恋花·伫倚危楼风细细》。意思为"我日渐消瘦也不觉得懊悔,为了你我情愿一身憔悴"。全句意象都需保留,译为"I never regret getting thinner with my clothes being looser than ever. For you I am thus pining away in deep yearning."。

14. "众里寻他千百度,回头蓦见,那人正在,灯火阑珊处",这句出自南宋词人辛弃疾的《青玉案·元夕》,意为"我寻找那人千百次,都没看见她,不经意间一回头,却看见了她立在灯火零落之处。""灯火阑珊处",译为"where the lamplight is fading"。全句译为"I have been seeking her in the crowd for numerous times. All of a sudden I turn around, only to find her where the lamplight is fading."。

(译注/顾韶阳)

朋 友 四 型
Four Categories of Friends

余光中

译/顾韶阳

译者按：本文是余光中于1972年5月发表的一篇散文，最初收录在《听听那冷雨》，由九歌出版社出版。作者选取了品质和趣味的双重维度，将朋友分为"高级而有趣""高级而无趣""低级而有趣""低级而无趣"四种类型，并逐一加以论述。语言诙谐幽默，直击人心，颇具洞见。

一个人命里[1]不见得有太太或丈夫，但绝对不可能没有朋友。即使是荒岛上的鲁滨逊，也不免需要一个"礼拜五"。一个人不能选择父母，但是除了鲁滨逊之外，每个人都可以选择自己的朋友。照说选来的东西，应该符合自己的理想才对，但是事实又不尽然。你选别人，别人也选你。被选，是一种荣誉，但不一定是一件乐事。来按你门铃的人很多，岂能人人都令你"喜出望外"呢？[2]大致说来，按铃的人可以分为下列四型：

One may not have a spouse in his lifetime, but never can he live without a friend—even Robinson Crusoe stranded on a deserted island is in need of a "Friday". One can't choose his parents, yet everyone, except Robinson, is free to choose friends. What is chosen is supposed to fulfill one's expectations; nevertheless, it is not always the case. You are to choose and to be chosen. To be chosen is an honor, but not necessarily a pleasure. With so many visitors ringing your doorbell, how could it be possible for each one of them to "surprise you by joy"? In general, those who ring your doorbell fall into four categories:

第一型，高级而有趣³。这种朋友理想是理想，只是可遇而不可求⁴。世界上高级的人很多，有趣的人也很多，又高级又有趣的人却少之又少。高级的人使人尊敬，有趣的人使人欢喜，又高级又有趣的人，使人敬而不畏，亲而不狎，交接愈久，芬芳愈醇⁵。譬如新鲜的水果，不但甘美可口，而且富于营养，可谓一举两得。朋友是自己的镜子。一个人有了这种朋友，自己的境界也低不到哪里去⁶。东坡先生杖履所至，几曾出现过低级而无趣的俗物？

第二型，高级而无趣。这种人大概就是古人所谓的诤友，甚至畏友了。这种朋友，有的知识丰富，有的人格高超，有的呢，"品学兼优"像一个模范生，可惜美中不足，都缺乏那么一点儿幽默感，活泼不起来。你总觉得，他身上有那么一个窍没有打通，因此无法豁然恍然，具备充分的现实感⁷。跟他交谈，既不像打球那样，你来我往，此呼彼应，也不像滚雪球那样，把一个有趣的话题愈滚愈大，精力过人的一类，只管自己发球，不管你接不接得住。消极的一类则以逸待劳，难得接你一球两球。无论对手是

The first category: the highbrow and humorous. Ideal as they are, friends of this kind are not so much sought for as chanced upon. There are as numerous highbrow men as there are humorous men, but men of both qualities are quite rare. While highbrow men arouse reverence, and humorous men, amusement, men of both qualities arouse unawed respect and unfrivolous amiability, with their charisma mellowing through increased communion. They are like fresh fruits, tasty and nutritious, achieving double effects of satisfying the taste buds and nourishing the mind. Friends are a mirror of one's own self. With friends of this kind, one can hardly sink into vulgarity. Were there any vulgar and boring men turning up where Su Dongpo (a great poet and essayist in the Song Dynasty) set foot?

The second category: the highbrow and humorless. These are probably what the ancients called the outspoken friends, or even the esteemed friends. Of them, some are with extensive knowledge, others noble character, still others a combination of both, exemplary like a model student. The pity is that without a sense of humor such a type seldom sparkles, as if one of the apertures in his head is blocked, rendering him somewhat muddle-headed and unrealistic. Talking with him is neither like playing tennis in which two players serve and hit the ball interactively, nor like the game of rolling snowballs in which an interesting topic grows through discussion. The energetic type keeps serving the tennis ball, regardless of your ability to hit it. The inactive type stands in front of the net at his ease, rarely hitting any ball from you. Be he energetic or inactive,

积极或消极,总之该你捡球,你不捡球,这场球是别想打下去的。这种畏友的遗憾,在于趣味太窄,所以跟你的"接触面"广不起来[8]。天下之大,他从城南到城北来找你的目的,只在讨论"死亡在法国现代小说中的特殊意义",或是"爱斯基摩人对性生活的态度"。为这种畏友捡一晚上的球,疲劳是可以想见的。这样的友谊有点像吃药,太苦了一点。

第三型,低级而有趣。这种朋友极富娱乐价值,说笑话,他最黄;说故事,他最像;消息,他最灵通;关系,他最广阔;好去处,他都去过;坏主意,他都打过[9]。世界上任何话题他都接得下去,至于怎么接法,就不用你操心了。他的全部学问,就在不让外行人听出他没有学问。至于内行人,世界上有多少内行人呢?所以他的马脚在许多客厅和餐厅里跑来跑去,并不怎么露眼[10]。这种人最会说话,餐桌上有了他,一定宾主尽欢,大家喝进去的美酒还不如听进去的美言那么"沁人心脾"。会议上有了他,再空洞的会议也会显得主题正确,内容充沛,没有白开。如果说,第二型的朋友拥有世界上全部的学问,独缺常识,这

it is you who are always picking up the ball, or else the game can hardly go on. What is disappointing about such a type of esteemed friends is that his scope of interest is too narrow to ensure a wider exchange of ideas between the two parties. In so big a world, he goes all the way from the northern end of the city to the southern end, only to discuss with you "the special significance of death in modern French novels" or "the attitudes of Eskimos toward sexual life". One can easily imagine how exhausting it is to pick up the tennis ball the whole night for friends of such kind. Friendship in this regard is as bitter as herbal medicine.

The third category: the lowbrow and humorous. Such a type is highly entertaining. He cracks the dirtiest jokes and tells the most plausible stories; he is the best-informed and the most popular; he has been to almost all fancy places and has played almost all nasty tricks. He is able to join in the discussions on any topic, and how he manages to do so is no business of yours, for all his learning is displayed in his efforts to conceal his ignorance from laymen. As to the professionals, well, how many professionals have you seen in this world after all? Therefore, he can hang out in various living rooms and dining rooms without showing his true colors. He has a glib tongue; with him at the dinner table, both the host and the guests will enjoy themselves to the full and the vintage wine in their mouths is less "refreshing" than the pleasing words in their ears. With him at the meeting table, the most pointless meeting seems to be meaningful with a sound theme and substantial content. If men of the second category have

一型的朋友则恰恰相反,拥有世界上全部的常识,独缺学问。照说低级的人而有趣味,岂非低级趣味,你竟能与他同乐,岂非也有低级趣味之嫌？不过人性是广阔的,谁能保证自己毫无此种不良的成分呢[11]？如果要你做鲁滨逊,你会选第三型还是第二型的朋友做"礼拜五"呢？

第四型,低级而无趣。这种朋友,跟第一型的朋友一样少,或然率相当之低。这种人当然自有一套价值标准,非但不会承认自己低级而无趣。恐怕还自以为又高级又有趣呢？然则,余不欲与之同乐[12]矣。

一九七二年五月

all the knowledge but common sense, men of this category are just the opposite: they have all the common sense but knowledge. Normally, a lowbrow person with humor is taken as a man of vulgar taste, so if you share pleasure with them, how can you avoid suspicion of being a man of vulgar taste? However, as human nature is varied, who can claim himself to stay totally immune to such vulnerability? Were you Robinson Crusoe, which category would you choose to be your "Friday", the third or the second?

The fourth category: the lowbrow and humorless. Friends of this category are as rare as those of the first, and the chances of meeting them are slim. They certainly have their own set of values by which they assume themselves to be highbrow and humorous. How could you expect them to admit they are lowbrow and humorless? In that case, I may as well avoid their company.

May 1972

▶ 注释：

1. "命里"没有译成"be predestined to have",而是处理成"in one's lifetime"。

2. "喜出望外",大多数人译为"be pleasantly surprised",译者借鉴 David E. Pollard 所译《尺素寸心》中的译文"surprise you by joy"。

3. "高级"与"低级","有趣"与"无趣"互为反义,译者选取了 highbrow/ lowbrow, humorous/ humorless,"高级""低级"表达趣味高雅或是低俗,"有趣""无趣"则表达有无幽默感。

4. "理想是理想",就是"尽管理想",译为"Ideal as they are","可遇而不可求"译为"not so much sought for as chanced upon"。

5. "敬而不畏,亲而不狎",大多数人直译为"be respectful but not awed, amiable but not frivolous"。译者尝试采用转移修饰词(transferred epithet),将其译为 arouse unawed respect and unfrivolous amiability。"交接愈久,芬芳愈醇"中"芬芳"一词较抽象,若直译则无法传达原文的思想内涵,结合上文应是指,"愈相处,愈觉得此人有魅力(charisma)",而这魅力随着不断的交往(increased communion)而更加醇厚(mellow)。

6. "境界也低不到哪里去"译为"can hardly sink into vulgarity", sink into 为处于某种(不好的)状态,"境界低下"实则为"品味低下",故译为 vulgarity。

7. "活泼"一词,译法颇多,译者几经斟酌,最后选了"sparkle"。《英汉大词典》中的解释为"(才智等)焕发,活泼;才气横溢"。此词旨在体现有幽默感的人活泼机智。"一个窍没有打通,因此无法豁然恍然,具备充分的现实感"译为"one of the apertures in his head is blocked, rendering him somewhat muddle-headed and unrealistic",其中,"窍"直译为"aperture","没有打通"译为"blocked","豁然恍然"反译为"muddle-headed",不"具备充分的现实感"是说这类人很迂腐,译为"unrealistic"。

8. "趣味太窄,所以跟你的'接触面'广不起来"译为"his scope of interest is too narrow to ensure a wider exchange of ideas between the two parties"。"接触面"这里指双方聊的话题,故译为"exchange of ideas between the two parties"。

9. 这句是典型的中文,以流水句一气呵成。原文有六个分句,而英文分句一般不超过三个,此处进行了语义上的合并,每两个分句一组,每组互相平行。Plausible 作"巧言令色、花言巧语"解,暗指"把没有道理的事情讲得貌似可信","消息"和"关系"未直译,处理成两个形容词 well-informed 和 popular,表达"消息灵通,关系广阔"之意。

10. "他的马脚"怎么会跑来跑去呢? 这里是一种部分代整体的修辞,在英文中还原成"他"跑来跑去(hang out),却不会显出其本来面目(true colors)。

11. "保证"未直译,处理为 claim oneself to…,即"宣称自己","毫无此种不良的成分"译为"stay totally immune to such vulnerability"。此处"成分"未直译,而处理成"vulnerability"(弱点)。

12. "不欲与之同乐矣。"译为"may as well avoid their company",即不相往来。

(译注/顾韶阳)

留住文字的绿意[1]
Retaining the Green through Words

董 桥

译/顾韶阳

译者按:这篇文章出自董桥于1999年出版的语文小品录《留住文字的绿意》,全文语言清新隽永,内容意味深长。董桥用诗般的语言感慨着万物之美,劝诫人们通过文字守住转瞬即逝的美丽,正如其在《留住文字的绿意》中所说的:"时代要有生机,语文要有新意,原则山水人文转眼都老得优雅不起来了。在文化意识上,我很怀旧,却也不甘心放纵自己化为数纸堆中的书蠹。我只希望在安装了空调设备的现代书房里,依然会有一盏传统的灯影照亮我的原稿纸和打字机。新和旧是可以同时存在的;多少前朝旧宅的深深庭院里,处处是花叶掩映的古树。房子和树是老的;花和叶是新的。"

前不久,我写《老同志,给我看一会儿!》[2],谈季羡林先生的一些新事旧事。我在文中说,季先生写过一篇文章记邻居一对老夫妇的小园,我说我没有读过这篇小品。读者沈秉和先生看了拙作[3],竟传来季先生的一篇《人间自有真情在》,说是收在季老[4]新篇《人生絮语》[5]中。文

Lately I wrote an essay titled "Old Comrade, Please Look after it for me!", which relates old and new anecdotes about Mr. Ji Xianlin. In that essay, I mentioned an article of his describing the small garden of an old couple next door and said I hadn't read it. Mr. Shen Binghe, upon reading my essay, sent me an article of Mr. Ji titled "There are Always True Feelings in the World", which, according to Shen, is included in the venerable author's new book *Random Talks about*

章开头说:"前不久,我写了一篇短文:《园花寂寞红》,讲的是楼右前方住着的一对老夫妇。"沈先生于是想到我说的那篇小品,应是《园花寂寞红⁶》了,是这篇《人间自有真情在》的姊妹篇。我非常谢谢沈先生的盛情;芜文引来这样可贵的心意,人间自不寂寞。

季先生说,这对老夫妇,男的是中国人,女的是德国人,在德国结婚后移居中国,都快半个世纪了。没想到一夜之间,男的突然死去,他天天莳弄⁷的小花园失去了主人,"几朵仅存的月季花,在秋风中颤抖、挣扎,苟延残喘⁸,浑身凄凉、寂寞。"那个小花园一定很幽秀⁹,园里连那些在北京只有梅兰芳家才有的大朵牵牛花都长得出来。季先生在那里住了三十年,从来没有见过老太太莳弄过花,"德国人一般都是爱花的,这老太太真有点个别。"¹⁰有一天中午,季先生看到老太太采集大牵牛花的种子:"她老态龙钟¹¹,罗锅着腰¹²,穿一身黑衣裳,瘦得像一只螳螂。"季先生问她,采集这个干什么?她说:"我的丈夫死了,但是他爱的牵牛花不能死!"。

Life. The article begins as follows, "Lately I wrote a short essay 'The Garden Flowers in Lonesome Crimson', telling of an old couple living in front of my house on the right." Mr. Shen was therefore convinced what I mentioned was none other than this one, "The Garden Flowers in Lonesome Crimson", a sister piece of "There are Always True Feelings in the World". I really appreciate Mr. Shen's kindness; the invaluable help my essay received from him signifies that there are always true feelings in the world.

Mr. Ji stated that the old couple, husband being Chinese and wife German, had been staying in China for almost fifty years ever since they moved to China from Germany after marriage. Who could have imagined the husband died overnight, and the garden he tended every day lost its owner, " with a couple of surviving China roses swaying in the autumn wind, struggling to prolong their last breath. They appeared gloomy and forlorn." That surely is a secluded and enchanting garden, where even grow huge morning glories which are thought to be found only in Mei Lanfang's garden in Beijing. For over 30 years, Mr. Ji had never seen the old lady looking after the flowers, "The Germans are generally flower lovers, but this old lady is an exception." One day at noon, Mr. Ji saw her collecting the seeds of the huge morning glory, "she wore a black dress, this doddering old woman with bent back, and looked as thin as a mantis." Mr. Ji asked her why she collected this, and she replied, "My husband was dead, but the morning glory he loved couldn't be so!"

老夫妇一儿一女都在德国,男的一死,老太太在中国是举目无亲了。她不会说中国话,吃不惯中国饭。"她好像是中国社会水面上的一滴油,与整个社会格格不入。"[13]但是,季先生说:"为了忠诚[14]于对丈夫的回忆,她不肯离开,不忍离开[15],我能够想象,她在夜深人静时,独对孤灯。窗外小竹林的簌簌声,穿窗而入[16]。屋后土山上草丛中秋虫哀鸣。此外就是一片寂静。"

季先生写这篇小品当是动了真情了,铺陈清淡[17],气氛温馨;最沉郁处,也只说:"茫茫天地,好像只剩下自己孤零一人。人生至此,将何以堪[18]!"我常想,世间花草树木最能体贴人心[19],现代都市高楼大厦林立[20],再不小心珍惜绿色生命[21],语言文字一定都随着枯死了。老先生平日莳弄花木,死后才有牵牛花陪着老太太孤守小园。窗外有了小竹林,晚来萧萧风过,老太太才听得到几声细语[22]。土山上长了草,自有秋虫说话。人间真情似乎都在园花园树之中,不然季先生也不会想写这两篇文章了。儿时故居后院矮篱边经常是牵牛花和西红柿交杂蔓生;池塘边是木瓜和杨桃;还有月

The couple's son and daughter were both in Germany, and with the death of the husband, the old lady was left alone and kinless in China. Unable to speak Chinese and unaccustomed to Chinese food, "she seemed a drop of oil on the sea of Chinese society, a social misfit." However, Mr. Ji added, "In order to cherish faithfully the memory of her husband, she decided to stay, for she couldn't bear the thought of leaving. I can imagine how she sat by the solitary lamp in the still of night. The rustle in the bamboo wood was penetrating in through the windows, and in the thick grass on the mound behind the house the autumn insects were chirping sadly. Apart from this, silence reigned."

Emotionally aroused as he was, Mr. Ji managed to narrate it in a measured tone and create a warm atmosphere. At its most depressed, the essay reads like this, "she seemed to be left all alone on this vast earth. What an unbearable existence!" I often believe that flowers and trees are most effective in soothing human souls; with a forest of skyscrapers emerging in modern cities, language will accordingly wither if we fail to treasure life of green. Only because the old man attended to flowers and trees when alive could his widow have morning glories keeping her company in the lonesome garden. Only because there was a bamboo wood outside the windows could the old lady hear the wind soughing and sighing in the quiet of night. Only because there was grass growing on the mound could she hear the chirping of the autumn insects. It seemed true feelings were shown in flowers and trees, otherwise Mr. Ji would never write such an article. In my

季和七里香。早岁园中读古书的情景至今难忘。后来旅英多年,花事更盛[23],青草深深,千红晒暖[24];夏季嗡嗡的蜜蜂早就成了记忆中不老的天籁。"Go where you will through England's happy valleys, deep grows the grass, flowers bask and wild bees hum"…

childhood, alongside the low hedge in the backyard of my house, morning glories intertwined with the vines of the tomatoes; by the side of the pond stood papayas and starfruits together with China roses and daphne odera. I could clearly remember how I read Chinese classics in the garden in my early years. Later I spent many years in England where flowers are in profusion: the grass grows deep and flowers bask in the sun. The humming of the bees in the summer lingering on in my memory is the eternal sound of nature. "Go where you will through England's happy valleys, deep grows the grass, flowers bask and wild bees hum"…

◆ 注释:

1. "留住文字的绿意"指用文字留住绿意,故译为"Retaining the Green through Words"。

2. 这篇文章出自董桥先生的《英华沉浮录》,讲述了衣着朴素的季羡林先生欣然答应帮把自己误认为老校工的北大新生看行李的故事。

3. "拙作"与后文中的"芜文"均为自谦说法,但由于英文中少有此表达,故译文中无须刻意译出"拙""芜"之意。

4. "季老"是尊称,译为"venerable author",这是对德高望重的季先生表示尊敬。

5. 《人生絮语》记录了季羡林先生在其耄耋之年回顾一生时总结出的种种人生感悟。"人生絮语"意为"人生漫谈",故可译为 Random Talks about Life。

6. 该题目原指园子里的花嫣红灿然却孤单寂寥,译者采取转移修饰语的手法,将其译为"The Garden Flowers in Lonesome Crimson"。

7. "莳弄"指照料花园,译为"tend""look after"或"attend to"。

8. "苟延残喘"本义指临死前勉强维持呼吸,译者将其译为"prolong their last breath",保留了原句中的拟人意味。

9. "幽秀"指清幽美丽,译为"secluded and enchanting"。

10. "个别"指例外,译为"special"则不妥,应译为"exception"。

11. "老态龙锺"指因年迈而步履蹒跚,"doddering"恰含此意。

12. "罗锅着腰"指驼背,译为"bent back"。

13. 译者保留了"中国社会水面上的一滴油"这一意象,译为"a drop of oil on the sea of Chinese society",同时将"与整个社会格格不入"译作同位语("a social misfit")进行补充说明。

14. 大多数人会将"忠诚"译为"be loyal to",但该译法与原词意有出入,且破坏了意境。"忠诚"在文中指珍爱、怀念,故译者将其译为"cherish faithfully"。

15. 译者采用反译法将"不肯离开"译为"she decided to stay"。此外,老太太"不肯离开"的原因在于"不忍离开",故译者将此句译为"she decided to stay, for she couldn't bear the thought of leaving"。

16. "穿窗而入"中的"穿"用以描绘声音穿透窗户的情形,故译者采用了"penetrate"一词,以体现声音的穿透力,且具有美感。

17. "铺陈清淡"指给人以娓娓道来之感,译为"in a measured tone",表示行文不疾不徐。

18. "人生至此,将何以堪"指此般生活难以承受,故译为"What an unbearable existence",该译法简洁凝练。

19. "体贴人心"指抚慰人心,译为"soothing human souls"。

20. 译者将"高楼大厦林立"译为"a forest of skyscrapers",既体现了数量之多,又保留了原句的比喻意象。

21. "绿色生命"指绿色具有活力,如有生命一般,译为"life of green"。

22. "晚来萧萧风过,老太太才听得到几声细语"一句中"细语"即指代"风声",故译者将"萧萧风过"与"几声细语"合并译为"the wind soughing and sighing in the quiet of night",其中"soughing"用以体现晚风飒飒之感,而"sighing"则保留了"细语"的拟人意味,且传递出一丝寂寥之感。

23. "花事更盛"指繁花尽放,译为"flowers are in profusion",以体现数量之多。

24. "千红晒暖"指花朵沐浴在暖阳下,译为"flowers bask"。

(译注/顾韶阳)

在敦煌时是与历史最亲近的时刻
——他与荒漠一见如故[1]
When in Dunhuang He Was Closest to History
—Love with the Wild at First Sight

作者:嘉穆

译/顾韶阳

译者按:这篇报道出自《新民晚报》,简要介绍了张岚军的作品展及其个人经历。全篇表达凝练而生动,行文如流水。

昨天,《势象——张岚军绘画作品展》在上海美术馆开幕。擅长铜版、水彩的张岚军用凝练的语汇,描绘出一路行走的足迹。前几个月还在川北流连的张岚军一开口,我们眼前仿佛也浮现出那些振奋人心的罕见风景[2],他轻柔的嗓音能立刻把你带入那个遥远的世界。如果不说他是艺术家,那你一定以为眼前是一位说故事的大师。

Yesterday, "Pattern of Momentum—Art Exhibition of Zhang Lanjun" opened in Shanghai Art Museum. Zhang Lanjun, who was adept in copperplate and watercolor, painted with concise language his footprints left in western China. The moment when Mr. Zhang, who lingered in North Sichuan several months ago, began to talk about his journey into the west, there emerged before our eyes thrillingly unusual views. His soft voice was able to guide the listeners into the depth of the remote world. He would have been taken for a master storyteller, had he not been known as an artist.

"说实话,我现在想起来还是阵阵害怕³,在那种人迹罕至的高原地区,恐惧是从心底最深处冒出来⁴的。有时候猛然一回头,看见一株狰狞的植物,真能让你毛骨悚然!但也有时,在满眼苍凉中忽然看到一处妖娆的景致,如一个美女般妩媚,那种感受只能体会,根本形容不出⁵!"回到上海以后,那些珍贵的记忆一泻而下,成就了张岚军画框里的任人浮想的杰作。⁶

张岚军尤其钟情那些荒凉之处,他称之为"气息吻合"⁷。在敦煌沙漠,他在夜半爬上高高的沙山,当含着沙的风从脸颊抚过,"什么都改变了,可那风还是和千年之前的一样,那一刻,是我与历史最亲近的时刻。"在《空山新雨》系列水彩画面前,那些异形异色的水彩块状真像是被施了魔似的,仿佛冉冉飘动的云彩。"不经受震撼,也震撼不了别人,艺术家啊,包括文学创作者,一定要多去感悟,多受震撼。"⁸他说。

酷爱洪荒漠野的张岚军,在铜版画上刻出了"古道西风瘦马"的意

"To tell you the truth, there have been pangs of haunting fear till today, for in those untraversed highland regions, fear welled up from the bottom of the heart. Sometimes when you turned around and, all of a sudden, caught sight of a hideously looking tree, you would be frightened to death. However, there were other times when you discerned a picturesque scene, as enchanting as a beauty, among all that bleakness, you could hardly describe it—such a scene could better be sensed than described." Upon returning to Shanghai, these cherished memories forced themselves out and found their ways into the appealing works of Zhang Lanjun.

Zhang Lanjun was particularly attached to the bleak places, which he termed as "places of affinity". In the desert of Dunhuang, he climbed up the high sand hill at midnight and let the wind with sand brush his face. "Everything has changed, but the wind has remained all the same for thousands of years. At that moment, I was closest to history." In the series of his watercolors entitled "Fresh Rain in the Hollow Mountains", those piles of watercolor with unique shapes and hues seem to be spelled, flowing like clouds. "You are unable to electrify the audience if you yourself have not been electrified. Artists, including literary artists, should experience epiphany and spiritual tremor," he said.

Zhang Lanjun, an ardent lover of desolate wildness, engraved on his copperplate the artistic

境,"断肠人在天涯"的苍凉结结实实地让人心生出无助、恐慌来[9]。可张岚军却把家定居在繁华都市。"我喜欢上海,喜欢它的热闹、时尚。但对我来说繁华是用来作对比的,只有感受到极度的繁华,才能更深刻地理解荒凉。"

ambiance of "a lonely man on a lean horse bracing the west wind on an ancient path into the edge of horizon", such solitude and desolation would surely send the audience into an abyss of helplessness and horror. Nevertheless, Zhang Lanjun settles down in the bustling metropolis. "I like Shanghai, its thriving and modern atmosphere. However, it is a matter of comparison: only when I have experienced the extreme thriving can I understand the deeper meaning of desolation."

于是,张岚军就那样选择了大隐于市[10]的生存和创作之道。"很奇怪,我在那么吵闹的地方,反而觉得心里很平静,很安全。那些潜藏在脑中的所有记忆自然而然就流露出来了。"[11]

Therefore, Zhang Lanjun naturally chooses to abode and paint in the hustle and bustle of the modern city. "It's strange enough that at such a clamorous place, I have a sense of inner peace and reassurance, and all the memories hidden inside find a spontaneous overflow."

注释:

1. "一见如故"形容初次相见就情投意合,在此文中的意思与"一见钟情"相近,故译者将其译为"Love with... at First Sight"。

2. "前几个月还在川北流连的张岚军一开口,我们眼前仿佛也浮现出那些振奋人心的罕见风景"一句中,前后两个短句的主语不同。若保留原句语序,则主从句主语变化太快,衔接不够自然。故译者将后半句倒装,以"there"一词自然承接前半句,最终将这句话译为"The moment when Mr. Zhang, who lingered in North Sichuan several months ago, began to talk about his journey into the west, there emerged before our eyes thrillingly unusual views."。

3. "我现在想起来还是阵阵害怕"指心有余悸,译者采用there be 句型将其译为"there have been pangs of haunting fear till today",其中,pangs 指阵阵痛苦,haunting 指萦绕心头。

4. "冒出来"用以形容某种情感迸发而出,译为"welled up"。

5. "但也有时,在满眼苍凉中忽然看到一处妖娆的景致,如一个美女般妩媚,那种感受只能体会,根本形容不出!"这句话短句较多,如何自然连接各分句并突出原句重点属一难点。大部分人会采用这种句式——"Sometimes when you suddenly saw…,your feeling could not be described but only be sensed."。该译法打乱了原句语序,美感缺失,无法传达出原文炽烈的情感。译者在遵循原句语序的基础上尽量保留其意境,将"那种感受只能体会,根本形容不出!"作独立主格结构处理并置于句末。这句话最终译为"However, there were other times when you discerned a picturesque scene, as enchanting as a beauty, among all that bleakness, you could hardly describe it—such a scene could better be sensed than described."。

6. "那些珍贵的记忆一泻而下,成就了张岚军画框里的任人浮想的杰作"指张岚军将涌入脑海的回忆注入其画作中,故译者将这句话译为"Theses cherished memories forced themselves out and found their ways into the appealing works of Zhang Lanjun."。

7. "气息吻合"在文中指张岚军对荒凉之处情有独钟,故译者将其译为"places of affinity",其中 affinity 指契合。

8. "多去感悟,多受震撼"指感悟万物真谛,受到精神震撼,译为"experience epiphany and spiritual tremor"。

9. "'古道西风瘦马'的意境,'断肠人在天涯'的苍凉"采用了互文手法,"意境"和"苍凉"看似各自指代"古道西风瘦马"和"断肠人在天涯",实则"'古道西风瘦马'的意境"和"'断肠人在天涯'的苍凉"互相渗透,互为补充,故译者将这句话译为"the artistic ambiance of 'a lonely man on a lean horse bracing the west wind on an ancient path into the edge of horizon', such solitude and desolation would…"。

10. "大隐于市"指在繁华都市中独善其身,译为"in the hustle and bustle of the modern city"。

11. "那些潜藏在脑中的所有记忆自然而然就流露出来了"中的"流露"为动词,很多人采用"reveal""reflect"等词来译"流露",未尝不可。此处译者将"流露"转译为名词"overflow",并用"spontaneous"来修饰该词,最后将这句话译为"all the memories hidden inside find a spontaneous overflow"。

(译注/顾韶阳)

那一刻，我看到了人性的光辉[1]
That moment, I glimpsed the glow of humanity

黄 柯

译/顾韶阳

译者按：《那一刻，我看到了人性的光辉》一文因上海"11·15"特大火灾而写，展现人性在面对生死时所显现的光辉。文中饱含着对死者的悼念，对人性的颂扬，令人感伤，发人深思。

2010年11月15日，上海，胶州路，一座大楼霎时化为一片火海[2]，几十条鲜活的生命[3]化为滚滚浓烟消逝而去，不知又为这人世增添了多少悲痛与苦难[4]。

第一天，不知在什么时间，也不知是谁所为，离那座大楼不远的路面上竟多了几株洁白的菊花。这些洁白的菊花在被熏得黝黑的建筑下，显得[5]安静而又自然。

第二天，几位路人驻足旁观，然后又留下几株菊花，默默离去。

On November 15th, 2010, a high-rise apartment building on Jiaozhou Road, Shanghai, was reduced in an instant to a sea of surging flames in which dozens of living beings vanished into nothingness, adding untold grief and pain to the world.

The first day after the fire, no one knew when and by whom a couple of white daisies were laid on the road near the building. These white flowers looked at ease and serene against the charred building.

On the second day, several passers-by stopped for a look; laying more daisies, they left in silence.

第三天，人越发多了起来，花也越发多了起来。

11月21日，死者的"头七"，街口警车停驻，警察手持对讲机不时联络，人群安静而平和[6]。胶州路上已经铺满了菊花，满眼皆白[7]。在沉默的鲜花和点点烛火之上，有一种安静、沉默却令人敬畏的力量在空气中散播，衬托着黑黢黢的死楼[8]，直立在即将落雨的天空。

开始是几个人，后来是几十、几百、几千人，死者"头七"那天，多达10万人来到现场悼念遇难者。上海城市交响乐团在入口处演奏的旋律轻柔优美的《圣母颂》在天空中飘荡，曲调中自有一股缓缓的令人安宁的力量[9]。它似乎充斥于天地，又似溢满于[10]心田；似对死者的度化，又似对人性的颂扬——它让人的灵魂得到真正的净化和提升。此时此刻，无论贫与富、善与恶，所有的一切都化为停驻的身影，化为对死者的哀悼，亦化为对生命的敬畏。在那点点烛火之上，看到烛光反衬的面庞，庄重、温暖而又协调[11]。

On the third day, more people gathered with more flowers laid.

On November 21st, the first seventh day of the mourning term, patrol cars parked at the street corner, and policemen were keeping in touch through intercoms. A solemn silence reigned among the crowd. White daisies stretching along the Road greeted the eyes. Over the quiet flowers and flickering candlelight, there floated in the air a life-force, silent, serene and awe-inspiring, against the blackened lifeless building under the gloomy sky of imminent rain.

The throng of the mourners was thickening with the increasing number, from tens to hundreds, then to thousands; and in the end, as many as 100 thousand mourners appeared on the sense. *Ave Maria*, a soft and sweet melody, played by Shanghai City Symphony Orchestra at the entrance, was in the air, exuding a tranquilizing force. The force, so to speak, permeated the universe and overflowed the human heart; it set the dead at rest and eulogized the glow of humanity: with it came the genuine purification and sublimation of human souls. At the very moment, the crowd, stripped of the distinction between poverty and prosperity, goodness and evil, fell into a concerted stillness aroused by a concerted mourning for the dead and a concerted reverence for life. The faces, revealed in the flickering candlelight, appeared grave, warm and congruous.

或许，人只有在面对死亡，在面对别人的最终宿命之时，才会显露出自己最真实的一面。人性本善，生活为人们披上了不同的外衣¹²，不见其本心，但"人禀七情，应物斯感"¹³，总会时不时地显露出其光辉。唯有超越世俗的羁绊，直接看到生命的最终站台，才会庄重，才会不分你我，才会发自内心¹⁴。

人性本善，其光辉一直在这痛苦的人世间感染¹⁵世人，如烛火，虽小却长存不灭，虽少却直达千万人心¹⁶，唯有真情流露之时，方可瞥见那光芒，如流水，如阳光。

人性的光辉，就在烛光映照面庞的那一刻，显得分外夺目。

Perhaps man is inclined to reveal his truest self only when faced with death, with others' loss of life. Man is intrinsically good, yet his true self is veiled by the harsh reality of mundane life. However, as the saying goes, "human emotions tend to be responsive to sensory stimuli", the glow of humanity shines through from time to time. Only when man looks beyond the earthly existence into the far end of life can he treat life with solemnity, with indiscrimination, and with utter sincerity.

Man is intrinsically good, and the glow of humanity radiates in the painful world, like candlelight, flickering yet inextinguishable, glimmering yet penetrating into the myriad human hearts. Only when one reveals his true self can he glimpse the very glow, flowing like water, shining like the sun.

The glow of humanity was exceptionally resplendent the moment the candlelight struck the faces of the mourning crowd.

▶ 注释：

1. 本文中"光辉"指人性之光辉夺目，译为"glow"。

2. "一片火海"译为"a sea of surging flames"，"surging"展现火势之大。

3. "鲜活的生命"译为"living beings"。

4. "不知多少悲痛与苦难"可理解为"无尽的悲痛与苦难"，"untold"一词即为"无尽的"，"难以言明的"。

5. "显得"即菊花在黝黑的建筑的衬托下显得安静又自然，此处"显得"可以用介词"against"表达"衬托"之意。

6. "人群安静而平和"意为人群笼罩在安静而平和的氛围中,因此译为"A solemn silence reigned among the crowd"。

7. "满眼皆白"有人译为"an eyeful of white",不妥,因为"have an eyeful of"是"一饱眼福"之意,与原文有出入,不如处理成"the white daisies greeted the eyes"。

8. 文中"死楼"表示楼中的人都已丧生,已再无生机,译为"lifeless building"。

9. "令人安宁的力量"实则为使人获得内心平静的力量,译为"tranquilizing force"。

10. "充斥于"译作"permeate",表"弥漫"之意,"溢满于"有充满之意,译作"overflow"。

11. "协调"一词译作"coordinate"和"harmonize"都不恰当,"协调"在此有些伤感的意味,不能译成正面意,"congruous"有"一致,协调"之意,用在此处更恰当。

12. 此处采取意译法,"生活为人们披上了不同的外衣"可理解为人的本心被现实的世俗生活所掩盖,译为"be veiled by the harsh reality of mundane life"。

13. "人禀七情,应物斯感"出自南朝文学理论家刘勰的《文心雕龙·明诗》,意为人有喜、怒、哀、惧、爱、恶、欲七种情绪,受到外界的刺激就会有不同的反应,译为"human emotions tend to be responsive to stimuli"。

14. "羁绊"没有直译为"fetter""yoke"之类的词,而是处理成"look beyond earthly existence"。"直接看到生命的最终站台"用一介词"into"相连,紧随上句,这样句子更为紧凑。"站台"大都直译为"platform",译者认为不如用"far end"更能体现"生命尽头"这一意象。"庄重,不分你我,发自内心"译者作了词类转换,处理成三个名词,用"with"引导"solemnity, indiscrimination, sincerity",效果不错。

15. "感染"译作"radiate"表示人性的光辉照耀人间。

16. "直达人心"表示人性之光辉有穿透人心的力量,译作"penetrate into","千万人心"译作"myriad human hearts","myriad"有"万千"之意。

(译注/顾韶阳)

细 艺[1]
Minor Hobbies

斯 人

译/顾韶阳

译者按：这篇文章是《读者》半月刊2016年第7期的卷首语。作者如挚友般向读者娓娓道来"细艺"的益处，并于文末得出了深刻的人生哲理——"人一生都应该有细艺"。从语言来看，全篇文白兼杂，零散结合；从布局来看，行文流畅连贯、由浅入深；从立意来看，该文蕴含哲理、引人深思。

一个朋友对我说：退休后要有一点"细艺"，"细艺"二字，真是传神[2]。

一种小小的兴趣，这就是"细艺"。退休后学点书法、打太极，拎部小相机周围[3]拍点有趣的照片，或者把丢了多年的二胡再拿出来练练，都是细艺[4]。

有人从小就集邮，坚持几十年，退休后当然可以继续；有人收集蝴蝶标本也养成长久兴趣，那也值得保持下去。

A friend of mine said to me that he would pursue a "minor hobby" upon retirement. How expressive the phrase is!

A small interest can be taken as a "minor hobby", such as what you enjoy doing after retirement: learning calligraphy, playing *Tai Ji*, taking photos of the scenes nearby with your little camera, or picking up the erhu that has been put aside for years.

Some have been collecting stamps for decades ever since childhood, and they should certainly go on with it after retirement. Others have developed a long interest of collecting the specimens of

细艺不需太多时间,也不要太费神,行之所欲行,止之所欲止[5],没有目的,没有野心[6],无关宏旨[7],有益身心。

　　做人不怕忙碌,只怕无聊。忙碌逼你好好安排时间[8],也能忙里偷闲[9];无聊时却不知如何是好[10],坐立不安。

　　明代袁中郎说:"每见无寄之人[11],终日忙忙,如有所失[12],无事而忧,对景不乐,即自家也不知是何缘故[13],这便是一座活地狱。""终日忙忙"当然是假象,就是好像有很多事做,但做的事都无趣,所以也不知自己在忙什么。更惨的是"无事而忧,对景不乐",简直了无生趣了[14]。

　　细艺可以填充你突然多出来的时间[15],不是什么正经事,做起来又可以很正经;虽然做起来很正经,却也不必抱着一种很正经的姿态去做。细艺的好处就是:它像是工作,又像是休闲,以工作的态度去休闲,又以休闲的方式去工作[16]。

butterflies, and such an interest should deservedly be sustained.

　　A minor hobby doesn't require too much time or energy—you can follow it as you please and stop doing so whenever necessary. It is pursued for no special purpose or with no undue expectations. It is trifling and is good for health.

　　Men fear tedium more than a busy schedule. A busy schedule forces you to spend your time properly so as to squeeze leisure activities in. However, tedium makes you disorientated and agitated.

　　Yuan Hongdao in Ming Dynasty said, "I often see those men of dreariness, though busy all day, feel as if disoriented; they look worried for no reason and feel distressed facing lovely scenes. With such an inexpressible mental state they live as if in a living hell." "Being busy all day" is of course a pretence: they seem to be engaged in piles of things that are dull and uninteresting, that's why they feel a sense of futility. What's worse, "looking worried for no reason and feeling distressed facing lovely scenes" suggest an intense apathy toward life.

　　A minor hobby helps fill the increased leisure; it is not something serious, yet it can be done seriously; though done seriously, it is not necessarily taken too seriously. The benefit of a minor hobby is that it seems both a job and a leisure activity; a leisure activity performed as if it is a job and a job done as if it is a leisure activity.

| 人一生都应该有细艺,不必等退休后。 | A minor hobby should be pursued throughout one's life, not necessarily after retirement. |

➤ 注释:

1. "细艺"原为粤语,由"细务"转变而来,指"细小的活动"或"技能",也就是用于消遣的活动。罗素在其著作《幸福之路》(*The Conquest of Happiness*)中曾用"minor interest"来解释"impersonal interest"(闲情逸致),译者认为"minor"一词与"细艺"中的"细"有异曲同工之妙,且适合修饰"hobby",故在翻译"细"时借用了该词。

2. "传神"指富有表现力,"expressive"的含义与其契合。

3. 若仅用一个副词"nearby"来翻译"周围",译为"taking photos nearby with your little camera",与原句含义相悖,且令读者迷惑,故译者增添"scenes"一词,译为"taking photos of the scenes nearby with your little camera"。

4. 这一段仅有两句话,且均以"细艺"结尾,故译者将两个"细艺"合并,并用"such as"来连接"细艺"与文中列举的各种退休活动,从而使译文更连贯,更紧凑。此外,译者增译"what you enjoy doing",既契合原文含义,又便于读者理解作者想要传达的意思。

5. "行之所欲行,止之所欲止"指按照自己的想法去做,不想继续的时候就停下来,译为"you can follow it as you please and stop doing so whenever necessary",以期达到简洁凝练、契合原文句式的效果。

6. 这里的"野心"意谓"期望过高",不宜直译为"ambition",可以译作"undue expectations"。

7. "无关宏旨"出自清代纪昀所著的《阅微草堂笔记·滦阳消夏录一》,指意义或关系不大,可译为"trifling"。

8. "安排时间"通常译为"arrange time"或"schedule time",但此文中的"安排时间"并非指做计划,而是指合理分配时间,故而译为"spend your time properly"。

9. 大部分学生会将"忙里偷闲"译为"从忙碌中挤出休闲时间",如"steal leisure time from a busy life",但这种表达不够地道。可以将"忙里偷闲"理解为"挤时间从事休闲活动"(squeeze leisure activities in),效果更好。

10. "不知如何是好"即晕头转向、没有目标,译为"disorientated"。

11. "无寄"指因心无所寄而郁郁寡欢,译为"dreariness"。

12. "如有所失"出自南朝宋刘义庆所著的《世说新语·德行》,指好像丢失了什么似的,形容心神不安的样子或心里感到空虚。此文中"如有所失"指因心无所寄而感到无所适从，译为"feel as if disoriented"。

13．"即自家也不知是何缘故"译成一个介词短语"with such an inexpressible mental state"，意为"在这样莫可名状的心理状态下"。

14．"简直了无生趣了"指生活没有滋味和乐趣，译者用"intense"来强调程度，用"apathy"来指代"冷漠""无生趣"。

15．"突然多出来的时间"即指多出来的休闲时间，故译者译为"increased leisure"。

16．"它像是工作，又像是休闲，以工作的态度去休闲，又以休闲的方式去工作。"这句话散句较多，且四个短句的主语并不相同，故如何连接四句话实属不易。多数学生会将"以工作的态度去休闲，又以休闲的方式去工作"直译为"doing leisure activities in the attitude as towards work and work in the relaxing way"，但这种表达不够地道，令读者迷惑，且难以衔接"它像是工作，又像是休闲"，故译者采用一定手法统一了四句话的主语，将后两个散句译为"a leisure activity performed as if it is a job and a job done as if it is a leisure activity"，该译句句式对仗，表达地道，且与前两个散句成平行结构，从而使行文连贯紧凑。

（译注／顾韶阳）

知 止[1]
Knowing When to Stop

草 白

译 / 顾韶阳

译者按：这篇文章出自《读者》半月刊 2015 年第 4 期的"点滴"专栏，作者是草白。"知止"，是中国哲学所独有的一种智慧，最早见于老子的《道德经》。作者在文中细数平淡生活里的种种"禁忌"，表达对"知止"这一人生境界的感悟和体味，全篇由浅入深，清新隽永。

小时候，立秋一过，家里人就不允许小孩去溪里玩水。哪怕酷热依旧，甚至比前几日更甚，也不可。好似立秋一过，水便无端端地[2]凉下来，再去水里嬉，寒意渗入体内，是要生病的。

小时生活在乡村的人总会得到许多教训[3]。不能对着月亮指指点点，做豆腐的时候不许聒噪，新年第一天的水存着不能倒掉，下颌牙掉了扔瓦楞[4]上，上颌牙掉了扔床底下，从晾衣绳的裤衩下

In my childhood, right after the Beginning of Autumn, we kids were not allowed to dabble in the stream, not even it was as hot or hotter than the previous days. It seemed as if the water, after this very day, would turn cool for no reason, and those who dabbled in it would feel a chill seeping inside and fall ill.

People who spent their childhood in the countryside would get a long list of do's and don'ts, such as don't point at the moon; don't clamor while making tofu; don't pour away the water on the first day of the lunar year; do throw the fallen lower teeth unto the roof, and the fallen upper teeth under the

钻过会长不高,晚上不能照镜子,老梳头会记性不好,纽扣扣错了是要打架⁵的,屋里打雨伞会成矮子,玩火者要夜溺,如此等等,没来由的禁忌,甚至带点迷信色彩,大都是正值兴高采烈之时,给人当头棒喝⁶,告诫不可忤逆放肆⁷。

  以致事到今日,当兴高采烈地行着某事,做着某梦,执着某念,便不时地有声音旁白⁸般响起,心底妄念尽消。有种被泼了凉水之感⁹,心陡然静下来。弘一大师有副字,就是"知止"两字¹⁰。知止比知足的境界更高一层¹¹,知足是不贪,知止是不随,不要,够了¹²。对烦恼和痛苦说够了,对财富和名望说够了,对安逸和欣悦也说够了。

  四时节气也在说止,说够了。夏天热够了,秋天来了。花开够了,便谢了。冬天冻够了,春风暖了大地。

bed; don't pass under the shorts hung on the clothes lines lest your growth be stunted; don't look into the mirror at night; avoid don't comb your hair constantly lest your memory should decline; don't wrongly button your clothes lest you be involved in fights; don't open an umbrella indoors lest you become a dwarf; don't play with fire lest you run into bed-wetting. All these taboos, though groundless and somewhat superstitious, served as head-on blows, i.e. timely warnings to those overjoyed against undue indulgence.

  The warnings were severe, so much so that even today when I'm joyfully doing a certain thing, or dreaming a certain dream, or dwelling on a certain idea, a voice always rings in my ear, dispelling all my delusions. My enthusiasm being thus dampened, I suddenly calm myself down. The eminent monk Master Hong Yi (Li Shutong) once wrote a piece of calligraphic work composed of two characters "知止" ("knowing when to stop"). Knowing when to stop is more demanding than contentment: contentment signifies "freedom from greed", while knowing when to stop signifies "no follow-up", "no more", or "enough is enough". As regards worries and pains, enough is enough; as regards wealth and fame, enough is enough; as regards comfort and joy, enough is enough.

  The four seasons also know when to stop, know enough is enough. When it's hot enough in the summer, autumn comes; when flowers blossom enough, they wither; when it's cold enough in the

知 止

winter, spring comes with its warm breezes caressing the earth.

老子也说,知止不殆,可以长久[13]。"止"字的甲骨文是一只鸟歇在树枝上,是羽飞乃止的"止"。而,心之所安即为止。

As the ancient philosopher Laozi puts it, "One who knows when to stop meets no danger, for that's the way to last." The character "止"(meaning "stop") inscribed on tortoise shells looks like a bird perching on the branch, indicating the stopping of a bird's flight. And, you know when to stop if you set your mind at rest.

注释:

1. "知止"一词在中国传统典籍中出现频率很高,含义各有不同,最早出自《道德经》第四十四章:"故知足不辱,知止不殆,可以长久",一般指懂得适可而止,译为"Knowing When to Stop"。

2. "无端端",同"无端",指(某一行为)没来由、毫无道理,故译为"for no reason"。

3. "教训",在文中并非表示"经验"或者"训斥"之意,结合下文提及的各种"没来由的禁忌",此处也应当理解为"该做或不该做的事",译为"do's and don'ts"。

4. "瓦楞"在此处指代"屋顶",在中国的传统文化中,"上牙掉了扔床底,下牙掉了扔屋顶",寓意期望上槽牙和下槽牙能按照各自的朝向快速生长,故将"瓦楞"直接译为"roof"。

5. 这是一种民间说法,认为扣错纽扣会使扣纽扣的人卷入纷争或者争斗,而不是纽扣本身,因此在翻译时需要明确指出"打架"的主体,从而使译文更清晰明朗;使用"don't"和"lest",能使译文平添一番对"禁忌"的忌讳和敬畏之心。

6. "当头棒喝",原为佛教用语,指佛教禅宗祖师对初学者,常不问情由,当头给以一棒,或大声喝叱以令回答,以考验领悟佛理的程度。后泛指促人醒悟的手段或给人严重警告,有学生译为"a sharp warning",倾向于将之意译为"严厉的警告",此处译者选用"head-on blows",更为形象贴切。

7. "忤逆放肆"指过分放纵,不受约束,译为"undue indulgence"。

8. "旁白"可理解为在耳畔响起,故未直译。

9. "泼凉水"英语有对应词"dampen"可用。

10. "有副字"指有副书法作品,译作"a piece of calligraphic work",而"知止"两字就是由"知止"两个汉字组成,译作"composed of two characters",注意"字"的不同译法。

149

11. 此处"更高一层"的表面含义是指"知止"的层次高于"知足",实际上是表示"知止"这一境界对人的要求比"知足"要高。若将"更高一层"直译为"a higher state",高下之分暗含贬义,稍显生硬,且与下文的结合不够紧密,故译者将其灵活译为"more demanding"。

12. "不随,不要,够了",简单明了地诠释了何为"知止"这一境界,表示不需要后续事物、不贪多、懂得适可而止。考虑到原文文字精练,译者在翻译时做了名词化处理,使译文同样短小精炼,且一一对应。特别是"够了"一词,还会在下文反复出现,为了体现译文的一致性,此处的译文必须要有很强的可搭配性,故译为"'no follow-up','no more',or 'enough is enough'"。

13. 出自《道德经》第四十四章:"故知足不辱,知止不殆,可以长久",意思是"懂得适可而止就不会遇到危险,这样才可以获得长久的平安",故译为"One who knows when to stop meets no danger, for that's the way to last"。

(译注/顾韶阳)

雪与炉火
Snow and Stove Fire

林国卿

译/顾韶阳

译者按：这篇文章出自《读者》半月刊2015年第16期的"文苑"专栏，作者林国卿。在文中，作者结合自己去西湖的所见所感，将清初名家张岱的《湖心亭看雪》中所描绘的西湖美景代入重现，虚实掩映间，文中美景与眼前美景重叠，时间的脉络也逐渐模糊，取而代之的是多重美的享受，全篇文笔清新自然，回味绵长。

西湖景点多、声名盛，我去之前印象较深的却只有苏堤、雷峰塔与湖心亭。记得苏堤是因为苏东坡，雷峰塔是因为白素贞，至于湖心亭，则是因为张岱的一篇小品文。

张岱这篇《湖心亭看雪》[1]只有两个段落，前段描写夜游湖心亭所见的雪景，后段写亭中遇见两人招呼饮酒。一写景，一写人，历来读者各有体会，有人说它是一种生活形

The West Lake is famous for many of its scenes, yet what impressed me most, before my first visit, were nothing but the Su Causeway, Leifeng Pagoda and the Mid-lake Pavilion. My knowledge of the Su Causeway was ascribed to Su Dongpo, my knowldge of Leifeng Pagoda, to Bai Suzhen, and my knowledge of the Mid-lake Pavilion, to an essay written by Zhang Dai.

The essay entitled "Enjoying the Snow at the Mid-Lake Pavilion" consists of two paragraphs: the first depicts the snowscape the author enjoyed during his night trip to the Mid-lake Pavilion, and the second describes his encounter with the other two visitors who

态,有人说它是一种孤独心境。我初读它时,却被文中连用的"一"[2]字所迷:"天与云、与山、与水,上下一白[3]。湖上影子,惟长堤一痕,湖心亭一点,与余舟一芥[4],舟中人两三粒而已。"[5] 这"一"字,写出夜景之寂静与作者之孤独,我因而当它是本文的"文眼"[6]。

张岱远望湖心亭只是"一点"[7],其实它是一个小岛,非只一亭。今年4月搭船游西湖,远看湖心亭,正好一叶小舟缓慢靠近小岛,岛上一座白色门墙立于湖水边,300多年前,36岁的张岱也许由此处登岸。

张岱到亭中后,亭里已有两人对坐,另有"一童子烧酒,炉正沸"[8],人声对话频频出现,已非前段之"人鸟声俱绝"。静谧变成热闹[9],画面色调也变了,上下一白出现了红点炉火,亭上两客惊喜,张岱自得,静谧气氛突转热络。读至此,文眼变成了"炉正沸"三字。张岱未取一砖一木,只用100多个字描绘了平常一夜,

invited him over for a drink. For centuries readers have tried to make different interpretations on the essay with its two paragraphs depicting scenes and people. Some take it as a portrayal of a lifestyle, while others regard it as a depiction of a lonely soul. When I read it for the first time, I was fascinated by the recurrence of "一(one, a or all)", "…with the sky, the clouds, the hills and the water all in white. What stood out in silhouette were a streak of the long causeway, a dot of the Mid-Lake Pavilion, a leaf of my boat and a few specks of the people in the boat." The character "一" which reveals the stillness of the night and the solitude of the author can be seen as the "keyword" of the essay.

The Mid-lake Pavilion Zhang Dai saw from afar was just a "dot", yet actually it was an islet, not just a pavilion. In April this year I went sightseeing on the West Lake. As I was gazing at the Mid-lake Pavilion, a small boat was nearing the islet where there's a white gate-wall by the side. 300 years ago, Zhang Dai, aged 36, might have gone ashore at this site.

Upon arriving at the pavilion, Zhang found two men sitting face to face and "a page keeping an eye on the boiling wine on the stove". Human voices and conversations took the place of "utter silence without sounds of men or birds." Stillness gave way to noise, and, with the change of the hues, all whiteness was set off by the red fire. With the two men being delighted, Zhang Dai being self-satisfied, the ambiance turned from silence into warmth. Here the keywords are "the boiling wine on the stove". Zhang

| 却为西湖另造一景,300多年未曾坍塌[10]。 | Dai managed to construct, not with a brick or a log, but with 100 words, a scene that remained intact for over 300 years. |

▶ 注释:

1.《湖心亭看雪》,选自明末清初散文家张岱的《陶庵梦忆》,全文不足二百字,却融叙事、写景、抒情于一体,用清新淡雅的笔墨,写出了雪后西湖的奇景和游湖人的雅趣。湖、山、游人,共同构成了一种画面感极强的艺术境界。此处标题简洁明了,因此直译即可,故译为"Enjoying the Snow at the Mid-Lake Pavilion"。

2. 节选自《湖心亭看雪》,此处的"一"作为文眼,首次在文中出现。由于下文通过一连串"一"组成的短语勾画了一幅绝美的雪景,且下文的"一"用法和含义各有不同,因此有必要在此处对"一"的含义进行重点和全面的阐释,故译成"one, a or all",清晰明了,兼顾全文。

3. 节选自《湖心亭看雪》,"上下一白",指天色湖光全是白皑皑的。一白,表示全白。一,表示全、都,故译为"all"。

4. 节选自《湖心亭看雪》,"长堤一痕,湖心亭一点,与余舟一芥",此处的三个"一"用法一致,描绘的景象分别是"西湖长堤在雪中隐隐露出的一道痕迹,湖心亭的一点轮廓,和一叶小舟",但三个"一"后各自缀有"道""点"和"叶",对应不同的景物,因此需要考虑量词的翻译,故译为"a streak of the long causeway, a dot of the Mid-Lake Pavilion, a leaf of my boat",对仗工整,恰到好处。

5. 节选自《湖心亭看雪》,"两三粒",指两三人,此处借人影写人,借人影小如豆粒大小来形容人的渺小,衬托天地之大。而实际上舟中除了游客还有船夫,因此此处的两三粒是虚指,故译为"a few specks of"。

6. "文眼",指文中最能揭示主旨、升华意境、涵盖内容的关键性词句,故译为"keyword"。

7. 节选自《湖心亭看雪》,此处的"点",是指人看向远方时,远方的景物在眼中宛如一个圆点。重点在于这个点是真实存在的,是可见的,因此有的学生译为"point"是不恰当的,而译成"spot"也不合适,"spot"或指一个真实的地点,或指一个斑点,与原文不符,故译为"dot"。

8. 节选自《湖心亭看雪》,"一童子烧酒,炉正沸",指"一个小书童正在烧酒,酒炉中的酒正在沸腾"。此处的"童子"类似于书童,译为"page"。

9. 节选自《湖心亭看雪》,"人鸟声俱绝",指"行人和飞鸟的声音全都消失了"。此处可理解为完全没有声音,万籁俱寂。尔后作者话锋一转,将景色拉到眼前,称"静谧变成热闹"。此"静谧"并非真的环境处于完全静谧状态,"热闹"也并非当下立即热闹起来,只是因为关注的角度在切换,所以景象也骤然不同,但角度的切换不代表景象的消失。因此不能简单地按照字面意思逐字翻译,故译为"Stillness gave way to noise"。

10. "300多年未曾坍塌",表达了作者对张岱在《湖心亭看雪》一文深厚描写功力的敬佩之情。全文不过100字,却构造了一个绝美的雪景世界,带给读者以跨越时间与空间的美的享受,原文用"未曾坍塌",而翻译时,如果直译,则稍显平平无奇,不出彩,可以反译为"remained intact"。

(译注/顾韶阳)